Quarto

First Published in 2021 by Motorbooks,
an imprint of The Quarto Group,
100 Cummings Center, Suite 265-D,
Beverly, MA 01915, USA.
T (978) 282-9590 F (978) 283-2742
Quarto.com

25 24   6 7

ISBN: 978-0-7603-6848-0

Digital edition published in 2021
eISBN: 978-0-7603-6849-7

Library of Congress
Cataloging-in-Publication Data

Names: Lewin, Tony, author.
Title: BMW M : 50 years of ultimate driving
    machines / Tony Lewin ; foreword by
    Jochen Neerpasch.
Description: Digital edition. | Beverly, MA,
    USA : Motorbooks, 2021. | Includes
    bibliographical references and index.
Identifiers: LCCN 2021015741 (print) |
    LCCN 2021015742 (ebook) |
    ISBN 9780760368480 |
    ISBN 9780760368497 (eISBN)
Subjects: LCSH: BMW M automobiles--
    History. | Sports cars--Germany--History.
Classification: LCC TL215.B25 L495 2021
    (print) | LCC TL215.B25 (ebook) |
    DDC 629.222/2--dc23
LC record available at
    https://lccn.loc.gov/2021015741
LC ebook record available at
    https://lccn.loc.gov/2021015742

*All images courtesy BMW AG PressClub and
BMW Archive except as noted otherwise*

Acquiring Editor: Zack Miller
Design: Cindy Samargia Laun

Printed in China

Frontispiece: Jeff Koons's BMW M Art Car
sits atop the *Preikestolen* (priest's seat) on
Lysefjorden fjord in Norway.

TONY LEWIN is a lifelong automotive
commentator and industry
analyst and has spent most of
his career testing cars, analyzing them,
and reporting on the ups and downs of
the global enterprises that build them.
He has been a regular writer and editor
for *Automotive News Europe* and
launched several pioneering titles
for *The Financial Times* as well as
contributing regular columns for other
national and international publications.
Today, Lewin divides his time between
journalism, books, and translation
work. His titles for Motorbooks include
*BMW Century, How to Design Cars
Like a Pro, The Complete Book of BMW,*
and *Speed Read: Car Design*. He also
translated *Junkyard: Behind the Gates
at California's Secretive European-Car
Salvage Yard* for Motorbooks. He lives
in East Sussex, England.

BMW M

50 YEARS OF THE ULTIMATE DRIVING MACHINES

TONY LEWIN
Foreword by Jochen Neerpasch

motorbooks

CONTENTS

FOREWORD

BY *JOCHEN NEERPASCH,*
Founding CEO of BMW Motorsport GmbH

IT WAS THE EARLY 1970s and Touring Car racing in Europe was booming like never before. I had been in charge of motorsport with Ford in Cologne since 1968, and we had developed our Capri into a highly successful competitor in the Touring Car series.

This was a time when BMW was entrusting its motorsports activities to independent specialist tuning outfits like Alpina, Schnitzer, GS, and Köpchen—teams that were developing the BMW Coupés themselves and entering them in the Touring Car series.

But those BMW Coupés were too heavy. With the teams doing their own development work, they found themselves competing with each other. That made it easy for us at Ford to win races and championships with our Capris.

Toward the end of 1971, Bob Lutz took over as sales and marketing director of BMW in Munich, a role that included responsibility for BMW Motorsport. As someone who knew full well how strongly success in motorsport could directly enhance the attractiveness of an automotive brand, Lutz must have been deeply unhappy to see his BMWs being beaten by the Capris.

This prompted him to phone me in January 1972, explaining that he wanted to restructure BMW's Munich-based motorsports effort. He asked me to help him in this reorganization, but he wanted to know: would I be prepared to take on a leading role in the new operation?

From my experience in the racing and high-performance sectors at Ford, one thing was immediately clear to me: a marque like BMW, with its traditions and image so closely associated with power and motor racing, should set up its own in-house motorsport organization. It should do more than simply build racing cars and enter them in races: it should also support the racing activities of BMW customers by developing and selling, in tandem, high-performance cars derived from motorsport models.

This led to a meeting in Munich and we quickly came to a deal. In May 1972 I took up my post as the first-ever chief executive of BMW Motorsport GmbH.

In those early years, the clear top priority of the company was to achieve success in motor racing. We built the thousand lightweight BMW CSL Coupés required for homologation, and we developed a competition version to be entered in races by our works team as well as tuner and customer teams. In our very first season of racing, our 3.0 CSL Coupés managed to clinch the hotly contested European Touring Car championship, and we were also successful in Formula 2 that season, with a March-BMW winning the European championship.

BMW Motorsport GmbH went on to success in many more motorsport disciplines and continued to chase new opportunities to broaden its reach. Among those that spring to mind are the Art Cars, the Junior team, the M1 and its Procar series, and the International Motor Sports Association (IMSA) series in North America.

The "man-machine" relationship has also been a key factor in shaping BMW Motorsport. Technologies developed in motorsport soon found applications in high-performance and standard production cars, and early on our racing drivers also began sharing their skills with BMW customers in the shape of driver training programs.

Neerpasch (seated on CSL, left) with BMW team drivers in 1973.

Jochen Neerpasch, right, with Hervé Poulain, who inspired the BMW Art Car series, in front of Jeff Koons's dramatic M3 GT2.

The man who started it all in 1973—Jochen Neerpasch pictured here in 2020 with BMW Junior Team drivers.

Even in those early years, in parallel with its main racing programs, BMW Motorsport GmbH began building the predecessors to the M5, upgrading small numbers of cars, and marketing them through the BMW dealer network.

The first car that was the exclusive handiwork of Motorsport GmbH was the M1. It was designed and developed by race car engineers as a "road-legal racing car." In my opinion, the M1 served as the foundation for the highly successful M GmbH we know today—not least because motorsport still plays a key role in the present-day range of BMW M cars.

To this day, M GmbH continues to develop race cars and enter them successfully in motorsports events. This rich vein of motorsport experience enables M GmbH to build unique, unmatched road cars such as the M5—cars that set racetrack lap times to equal those of competition cars, but which give

the driver the comfort of a large limousine for their return journey home.

To produce such distinctive, remarkable cars—cars that are vastly more than a mere means of transport—it takes a close connection to motorsport, and it takes an organization like BMW M GmbH.

Even in today's rapidly changing time of heightened environmental awareness, BMW M GmbH will continue to deliver products that retain the legendary BMW magic, cars that give their owners the most precious of gifts—sheer driving pleasure.

I am delighted to pay tribute to BMW M GmbH, now with fifty years of proud history behind it and which still builds the pure-blooded BMWs that I so treasure.

Neerpasch (driver's side) at the Norisring M1 Procar Revival in 2019, with Harald Grohs.

Neerpasch is interviewed at the Blue Hero art installation celebrating his years with BMW.

THE
POWER
TO WIN

1

Inside the
performance
culture of
BMW's
M Division

Then and now: just as with the legendary
M3 of the 1980s, BMW M division continues
to develop exhilarating machinery for
keen drivers.

▲▲ An active involvement in top-level motorsport has always been central to the success of BMW's high-performance road cars.

▲ *M* is the most powerful letter in the world. Who could argue with that?

IT IS OFTEN ASSERTED, not least by BMW itself, that *M* is the most powerful letter in the world. That may smack of Madison Avenue advertising bluster, but behind the headline swagger there lie more than a few grains of truth—especially if the frame of reference is all things automotive.

After all, you don't have to be a fully committed auto fanatic for the combination of the letter *M* and the figure *3* to strike a chord or even quicken the pulse. But who, aside from complete car buffs or forensically focused magazine editors, could in all honesty picture an RS4, let alone realize it's an Audi? Or who would have heard of AMG were it not emblazoned on the flanks of Lewis Hamilton's multiple-championship-winning Mercedes Formula 1 car? And what, if anything, is an SVR?

Yet most of these premium sub-brands, it could be argued, have been set up in direct response to the success of BMW and its M—for Motorsport—division. And the explosive growth of this M enterprise is itself a subset of a much wider auto industry phenomenon: the unstoppable advance of the premium segment over the past four decades, triggered in no small measure by BMW's invention of the affordable, sporty, high-quality car in the 1960s. M has raised the original BMW brand promise to an even higher level, capitalizing on the solid sporting reputation the company built during the first quarter of its hundred-year history.

The BMWs of the 1960s and 1970s that powered the company's spectacular postbankruptcy turnaround were impeccably engineered, fun to drive, and not excessively expensive. This made them not only a refreshing contrast to their stodgy, stuck-up rivals, but also the ideal basis for racetrack competition. Handled by privateers at first, but with the tacit assistance of talented in-house engineers as the campaigns developed during the 1960s, BMW's motorsports program was rewarded with multiple Touring Car championships toward the end of that decade, making the natural next step the formalization of an in-house competitions department, BMW Motorsport GmbH. The creation of this division, in May 1972, marks the official start of the M story.

The principal landmarks of that story are the stuff of motorsport legend: the thundering CSL Coupés that swept all before them on 1970s racetracks; the explosively powerful Formula 1 engine that won the 1983 World Championship; the early production cars such as the exotic M1, the serial race winner for the road that was the original M3; and the pedigree bloodline of fabulously fast road cars that the M3 sired.

This car, along with its equally rapid but less rowdy running mate, the M5, went on to establish the anchor points for a dynasty that, over the course of fifty years, has expanded from two to a dozen or more models, swelling sales from a few hundred each year to over forty thousand—or more than a hundred and forty thousand if the less extreme M-Performance models are also included. In that time the division's head count has mushroomed from a tiny nucleus of race specialists to a nearly four-figure cohort of engineers, designers, programmers, marketing specialists, and motorsport professionals.

But why has the M venture been so consistently successful over so many years? And why has it attracted so many imitators, everywhere from nearby Stuttgart and Ingolstadt to faraway Coventry, Nagoya, Seoul, and even Detroit?

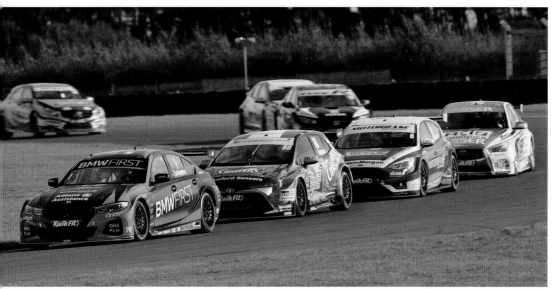

▲ Le Mans winners old and new:
BMW's victorious 1999 car alongside
the diminutive Touring-bodied 328, which
finished a remarkable fifth overall in the
1939 event.

◄ Participation in national race series
is important to BMW too. Here, Colin
Turkington's 330e leads the pack in the
2020 British Touring Car Championship.

First and most obvious, the division has been responsible for a long line of fabulous
high-performance sports cars, sedans, and SUVs, all selling strongly and at distinctly
premium prices. This has effectively built up a worldwide fan base of devoted
enthusiasts, all of them eager to lay down healthy deposits to subscribe to each new
chapter in the story.

Markus Flasch, CEO of BMW GmbH and seen here on the left, and Dr. Markus Schramm, head of BMW Motorrad, with the new 2021 M3 and M4 on either side of M's first motorcycle, the 212 horsepower M 1000 RR.

As for the success of the cars themselves, that is attributable fair and square to one thing: their authenticity. Without exception, they are the real deal: they perform brilliantly and are thrilling to drive. Right from the get-go with the M1 and the M3 in the 1980s, the M production cars have enjoyed a unique, hard-wired, symbiotic relationship with their opposite numbers on the racetrack. This two-way, win-win interface with the motorsport community is the envy of every other automaker, and is uniquely able to distill success on the circuits into an exhilarating driving experience for customers on the road.

Race Car to Road Car: That Unique Connection

In documenting the advance of BMW's M business over the course of half a century, it is clear that, early on, BMW Motorsport GmbH (its original name) had hit upon a formula unique in the auto industry at the time—a formula that also proved unique in its capacity to endure and to further evolve with each succeeding generation of models.

BMW's all-important realization back in the 1970s was that there was an unfulfilled desire among discerning customers for models that could deliver extreme performance, but without the exhibitionism, the tricky temperament, and the discomfort that tended to spoil aftermarket tuning packages. This was the perfect extension of BMW's core brand position of sportiness, style, and quality—especially as the company soon recognized that those same customers were prepared to pay a hefty premium (sometimes even double the price) for the trustworthy, top-quality engineering that would deliver this hitherto unavailable combination of qualities. The M philosophy has always been intrinsically bound up with the division's motorsport origins and the exclusivity that derives from the team spirit of the global motorsport community. This in turn feeds the broader team spirit among the M Division's now eight-hundred-strong specialist workforce, as today's CEO Markus Flasch relates: "Very many of the people we employ here in Garching are keen drivers; lots of them are motorsport experts themselves and lots also do customer racing track days. They have their own cars at home, they have their own garages. We have high-performance people here and it's a high-performance culture.

"People who work at BMW M live and breathe what they do," he continues. "Each and every car we put on the road is developed on the Nordschleife—the Nürburgring is very close to [good] public roads. This is why our cars are outstanding on normal roads—and on racetracks."

The high-performance culture that is the order of the day at BMW M can be a tough taskmaster, especially with rival brands snapping ever closer at M's heels: whereas classic M models such as the E46 M3 used to have the elite high-performance field all to themselves, today's equivalent, the G82 M4, can count three or more direct competitors eager to snatch its crown. Just as in motorsport, it is a race to stay ahead of the pack: boundaries must be pushed, or smashed, ingenuity and inventiveness must be turned up to the max, and anyone who pauses for breath will find themselves at the back of the field. But, most of all, BMW's toughest challenge is the one it has set itself: the most sacred ground rule within the M Division is that every new model must outperform the model it replaces.

This is none too easy when it is something like a 630 horsepower M5 scheduled for replacement, but performance can be defined in a variety of ways—not necessarily just horsepower. The ingenuity of engineers, especially M engineers, knows no bounds and, says Markus Flasch, they will rise to any technical challenge. One such challenge presented itself just after the turn of the millennium as BMW product planners began weighing the possibility of an M version of the X5 and X6 SUVs. To many people outside the organization, the very idea of a sporting SUV seemed logically impossible. To M engineers, though, the problem was not a philosophical one, simply the technical challenge of making a near two-ton, high-riding off-road-capable vehicle perform like a sports car. And when the X5M and X6M appeared in 2009, all agreed that it was mission accomplished.

Nowhere will ingenuity and new solutions be more important than when preparing for the future, both short and medium term. The escalating global climate challenge and tightening emissions legislation suggest the days of the CO_2-emitting combustion engine are now numbered—and for BMW this threatens the very technology that does so much to define the character of every M Car and the brand's technical allure for customers, commentators, and fans.

Jochen Neerpasch, left, inspiration behind BMW's M adventure, and Markus Flasch, the man who runs it today.

Yet the transition to zero-emissions power holds no fear for Flasch and his M colleagues. All exude the calm confidence that the M ethos of innovation and constant improvement will help them push even more powerfully into the era of net zero, ensuring that the thrill of driving never goes out of fashion—even if emissions are off the agenda and autonomous robots threaten to take over the driving tasks that we so enjoy.

Fanciful thinking? Perhaps not. As the chapters that follow will show, the M GmbH engineers and the confident, can-do culture of the whole organization have succeeded in keeping BMW ahead of the performance car field for fifty years—and there is every indication that this momentum can be carried through into the new zero-carbon world that awaits us all.

MOTORSPORT
IS IN *BMW'S* BLOOD

2

A century of success on two wheels and four, in F1, Touring Cars, Le Mans— and in the air

An early fruit of BMW's motorsport involvement was the explosively powerful 2002 Turbo of 1974. Unfortunately its arrival coincided with that of the first fuel crisis, cutting its career tragically short.

▲▲ Premier league winner: BMW powered Nelson Piquet's Brabham to the F1 World Driver's Championship in 1983.

▲ The Championship-winning M12/13 still stands as the most powerful engine in F1 history, but was developed from a standard road car unit.

A WARM SPRINGTIME AFTERNOON in South Africa's northeastern Transvaal province—and BMW is just about to grab the prize that has been its goal for so many years.

It is October 1983, Lech Walesa has just won the Nobel Peace Prize, *The Right Stuff* is about to hit America's movie theaters, and "Total Eclipse of the Hear" and "Karma Chameleon" are at the top of the singles charts. It also happens to be the final race of a tightly fought Grand Prix season, with three drivers in with the chance of snatching the Formula 1 World Champion's crown.

After a nail-biting ninety minutes of hard-charging racing over seventy-seven laps of the Kyalami Grand Prix circuit, it is Brabham-BMW driver Riccardo Patrese who takes the checkered flag, still pursued by a fast-accelerating Andrea de Cesaris in his Alfa Romeo.

But the biggest cheer comes as Nelson Piquet cruises home in third place, also in a Brabham-BMW. A fresh-faced thirty-year-old from Brazil, he has just clinched his second World Championship title and, after the Champagne has been sprayed and the hubbub subsided, he says he hopes he'll go on to win more.

For the Formula 1 world, this is a significant technical milestone: the first time any driver has won the Word Championship in a turbocharged car. For BMW, however, it is an even bigger deal. As a firm with "Motor" as its middle name and with a lifelong involvement in motorsport, it is an immensely symbolic moment and the culmination of everything the company culture stands for. To design, develop, and successfully race a top-level Formula 1 engine is honor enough; but for that engine to be in the back of the car that goes on to propel a top-line driver to the World Championship in motorsport's premier league is the crowning achievement—and just about the highest summit an engine maker can aspire to.

The Winning Mindset

Amid the euphoria it mattered little at that stage that the company had failed to clinch the Constructors' Championship at the same time—that would follow in the next season or two, it was reasoned. What really mattered was that BMW could now stand with justifiable pride on the top step of the podium and be regarded with just as much respect as its avowed rival, Mercedes-Benz.

That was of particular importance to the man who had done so much to raise BMW up to this elevated level: visionary CEO Eberhard von Kuenheim. Already twelve years into his tenure, and with his grand plan to square up to Mercedes already running ahead of its targets, von Kuenheim was cautious in detail but at the same time highly ambitious when it came to the bigger picture. Production had nearly tripled under his watch so far, the second generations of the super-successful 3- and 5-Series were in high demand, and a stunning new 7-Series was in development for launch in 1986. What von Kuenheim but few others at that time knew was that that 7-Series would conceal a remarkable trump card, one designed to deliver a body blow to Mercedes where it would hurt most—in the three-pointed star's perceived exclusive domain of supreme luxury and sophistication. It was to be nothing less than a V-12 engine, the first in a German production car for half a century, and it would demolish forever the notion that Mercedes-Benz had a monopoly when it came to delivering the ultimate in engineering accomplishment. As such, creating the engine powering Piquet to the World Championship in motorsport's pinnacle class played perfectly into BMW's agenda of being the world's best automotive engineers.

◣ The F1 winning team, from left to right: Nelson Piquet, engine guru Paul Rosche, and design mastermind Gordon Murray.

▼ CEO Eberhard von Kuenheim's strategic plan saw BMW become a major player in the global automotive industry.

Yet to say that it had been a long hard slog to reach this elevated status would be something of an exaggeration. Yes, it had taken several generations since the firm that was to become known as BMW was founded in 1916, and the company had grown and changed beyond all recognition. But as a corporate culture, even in its early aero-engine years, BMW was a competitive enterprise that was accustomed to winning—and, even then, that winning mindset provided an innate confidence to explore innovative ideas and to put them into practice to fly further, faster, and higher than everyone else. Quite literally so, in fact.

Further, Faster, Higher

In the years immediately following World War I, armistice conditions expressly forbade BMW from building its six-cylinder aero engines, engines that had become legendary thanks to their success in the Fokker D V.II in aerial dogfights over the western front. But there was nothing in the rules that prevented those same engines from being developed and improved—and this is what Max Fritz, the gifted engineer behind the Type IIIa and Type 4 (and soon the remarkable R32 motorcycle) proceeded to do.

By systematically improving the already innovative carburetor feeding the 19-liter unit, Fritz was able to extract more power and, more importantly, enhance its high-altitude performance to raise its service ceiling. In a series of well-publicized flights in 1919, Frank Zeno Diemer, a test pilot for Dornier, broke numerous international altitude records with BMW power, including 9,760 meters in the DFW37/III biplane and, remarkably, a passenger-plane high of 6,750 meters in a Junkers Ju F.13 monoplane with eight people aboard.

In a sign of what was to come in the next chapters of its history, BMW quickly capitalized on these achievements, promoting its competitive edge with a series of elegant posters that are familiar to this day. As something of an aside, these

BMW's expertise in high-performing power units was honed in the aero engine sector, where the company achieved numerous altitude records.

posters gave rise to what has become a widespread misconception about the BMW logo, that the blue-and-white roundel represents the spinning propeller of an aircraft. Nor do the blue and white represent air and water, another suggestion based on the period when BMW produced marine engines. Instead, and more prosaically perhaps, the blue and white are the official colors of the Bavarian state where BMW is based—except that the colors are reversed as, when the logo was registered in the 1920s, local trademark law did not allow the use of the state coat of arms for commercial purposes.

BMW's competitive streak soon found further expression at zero meters of altitude—on two wheels. Max Fritz's flat-twin R32 had astonished the motorcycle world on its debut in 1923, and a steady stream of engineering improvements delivered more power, better performance, and, inevitably, the desire to race and win. Instrumental in this was Ernst Henne, who joined BMW as a works rider but quickly displayed a multitude of other talents: as well as winning national championships in several classes, he led and inspired BMW's campaign to set motorcycle land-speed records on Germany's newly opened Autobahns. He was an accomplished master in the International Six Days Trial, at that time a major fixture in the motorcycle calendar, and on four wheels he won the 1938 Eifelrennen on the Nürburgring in the brand-new BMW 328 sports car on its first-ever outing.

And it is the handsome two-seater 328, with its advanced and innovative overhead camshaft six-cylinder engine, that can be recognized as the first product of an inventive, highly productive hothouse culture that was unique to BMW. That culture grew out of the intensity of international motorcycle racing, where the people who

Innovation on two wheels: the R32 stunned the motorcycle world in 1923 as the first truly modern and integrated design. Its boxer motor layout is still in high demand with today's BMW enthusiasts.

designed and engineered the bikes were often those who drove to the circuits, raced, and won on the weekends. But crucially, though this impetus would be interrupted by the horrors of World War II and the chaos that followed, this was the very same spirit that saw the newly prosperous BMW of the 1960s take to the racetracks again. Before long, these successes would crystallize into a formal motorsports entity—BMW Motorsport and, later, BMW M GmbH. This in turn would go on to the still greater heights of international Touring Car racing, Formula 1, Le Mans, and world endurance rallying. And, of course, to all the high-performance M-badged production cars that we now know so well.

The stylish 328 Roadster set the template for future M Cars: light, fast and agile, entertaining on the road, and a race-winner straight out of the box.

▼ The technically advanced 328, here with streamlined bodywork by Touring, was BMW's first truly successful competition car.

▲ Alexander von Falkenhausen, left, and Paul Rosche: architects of BMW's motorsport successes all the way from motorcycles to Formula 1.

An Aristocratic Genius with a Winning Streak

But back, for the moment, to the early 1930s, when the real seeds of BMW's M operation were sown. One personality in particular stands out: an aristocrat who not only was a highly talented motorcycle racer and car driver but who also displayed a remarkable aptitude for chassis and engine design and, later, for organizing whole competition departments and engineering programs to deliver success on the racetrack. It is no exaggeration to say that this individual was one of the greatest influences—alongside Eberhard von Kuenheim—in shaping BMW's history and establishing the high status it enjoys today. When he finally stepped back from BMW in the late 1970s, well beyond the stipulated retirement age, he was the company's oldest employee bar none and could look back on a lifetime of constant engineering innovation, motorsport victories, and success where it counts most of all—among customers flocking to BMW showrooms.

Baron Alexander von Falkenhausen first came to the company's attention as a seventeen-year-old whose racing prowess on a variety of motorcycles worried BMW's own team of riders. In 1934, after he had graduated from university as a mechanical engineer, he joined BMW as a works rider and designer, initially in the area of frames (where he helped develop the first telescopic front forks) and soon also in engine design.

By now already a highly regarded motorcycle manufacturer, BMW was also becoming established in the car business with an initially license-built version of the British Austin 7. This fragile lightweight was systematically improved by BMW and renamed

The elegant 507 sports car of 1955 has become an icon of the BMW marque but its high price and exclusivity precluded a competition career.

Dixi; a factory-backed team of three 748cc 3/15 models even won the 1929 Alpenpokal, the forerunner of the Alpine Rally. Von Falkenhausen bought and raced a series of BMW models, culminating in a 315/1 roadster (which by now boasted a six-cylinder engine) and scored several successes in circuit races and hill climbs. It was this symbiosis among racetrack, competition department, and production car development that proved so decisive in the creation of the sensational 328, the elegant but devastatingly potent two-seater roadster that was a winner straight out of the box when the prototype broke cover in 1936.

From an original output of 80 horsepower, already impressive for the time, the 328 was systematically developed until it was giving over 136 horsepower on special racing fuels. It won 130 races between 1936 and 1940, including class wins in the 1938 24 Hours of Le Mans and the Mille Miglia. The following year, a 328 with special aerodynamic aluminum bodywork by Touring of Milan finished fifth overall at Le Mans and took overall victory in the 1940 Mille Miglia; additional 328s finished third, fifth, and sixth, underlining the progress made by BMW's racing specialists.

The value of the direct link between motorsport and production cars was quickly taken onboard by all concerned, and this became the modus operandi for BMW's performance-model development thereafter. After the war, von Falkenhausen went on to win races and championships in BMWs run under his own team colors. After some success in the 2-liter Formula 2, he rejoined BMW in 1954 to manage the racing division and guide engineering development of the racing motorcycles. By 1957 he was put in charge of all engine development, including the flat-twin units powering the 600 four-seater bubble car—an example of which, implausibly, he even rallied.

That engine, which had begun life as a motorcycle unit, was especially potent in the back of the pretty 700 Coupé. Again, von Falkenhausen himself—along with future star drivers such as Jackie Ickx, Hubert Hahne, and Burkard Bovensiepen—campaigned the lightweight 40 horsepower 700 with great success in both circuit races and rallies, collecting a fifth place overall in the prestigious Monte Carlo rally in 1961 and the European Touring Car championship in 1963.

By this time, BMW was safely past the existential crisis of its late-1959 rescue from financial bankruptcy. In the safe hands of white knights Herbert and Harald Quandt, the company now enjoyed the luxury of longer-term business and product planning. Here again, von Falkenhausen played a key role alongside Paul Rosche, who led the development of an advanced, all-new high-performance engine earmarked for the breakthrough Neue Klasse sedan.

Yet not even these brilliant engineers could have imagined the remarkable success the M10 engine would go on to become: multiple millions would be made over a near thirty-year production life span. A quarter century later it would power the legendary M3, winning the Formula 1 World Championship and going down in history as the most powerful engine in Formula 1's hall of fame with an incredible 1,400-plus horsepower from just 1,500cc.

M10: The Engine That Turbocharged BMW

But we are jumping ahead again. Back in 1961, the specification of the new M10 engine was advanced for its day but gave little sense of the remarkable future the powerplant would enjoy. Rosche and his team ensured the four-cylinder aluminum-head design had the very best basics to ensure plenty of scope for further development: a five-bearing crankshaft for smoothness, a chain-driven overhead camshaft for durability, and enough space between the bore centers to allow for later expansion from its initial 1.5 liters to 2 liters or more.

The "Neue Klasse" sedans of the 1960s marked a turnaround in BMW's fortunes, both commercially and on the racetracks. Here, Hubert Hahne makes a pit stop in the 1966 Spa 24 Hours in the 2000ti he shared with Jackie Ickx.

Key to the success of all BMW models from the 1960s onwards was the advanced overhead camshaft M10 engine, masterminded by Paul Rosche. This is the later Turbo version, developed with know-how gained in Touring Car racing.

"As the man responsible for design and development, von Falkenhausen had to fight his corner in some tough debates with the BMW board over the apparent extravagance of the five-bearing crankshaft, the overhead camshaft, and the unusual combustion chamber design," recalls the company's official tribute to their engine boss, later to be described as a "human combustion chamber" by the respected Swiss magazine *Automobile-Revue*.

By the following year, the 1500 sedan was in full production and before long there was a 1600 version and then an 1800, now giving 90 horsepower for sparkling performance. The M10's potential was becoming clear: twin Solex carburetors eased horsepower up to 110 in the 1800 Ti, but the really big move came at the end of 1964 with the 1800 TiSA. This was one of the earliest examples of a homologation special—a special high-performance version built in limited numbers to enter Touring Car race series. In BMW's case, the 1800 TiSA was a model developed with the express intention of scoring big-league overall race wins rather than just class victories.

Some 30 percent more expensive than the model it was based on, the 1800 TiSA offered no fewer than 130 horsepower thanks to its twin Weber carburetors, larger valves, a very high compression ratio of 10.5:1, and a special camshaft developed by Paul Rosche, who by now was rejoicing in the affectionate nickname *Nocken-Paul* or "Camshaft Paul." To complete the engineering specification there was a five-speed gearbox—again an exotic rarity at the time—to take the drive to a limited slip differential on the rear axle, as well as uprated brakes and wheel bearings, and a quicker steering box. Inside, there were race-style bucket seats, a wood-rimmed steering wheel with slotted bright-metal spokes, and an add-on rev counter (red-lined at almost 7,000 rpm) placed centrally on the dashboard between the speedometer and the combi instrument.

All in all, the TiSA was the closest thing on the market to a circuit-ready racer, and its impact was instantaneous. With a top speed of almost 190 kilometers per hour and 0–100 kilometer-per-hour acceleration in less than nine seconds, it offered pretty sensational performance—all in a package refined enough for everyday use and seating five in comfort. All two hundred were sold in short order, and in every sense the TiSA can be seen as the true precursor of the six generations of M5 we know today.

The TiSA began its winning ways right away, driven by stars like Hubert Hahne and Rauno Aaltonen and starring in an epic duel with a mighty Mercedes 300SE in the 24 Hours of Spa in its debut year, taking the win the following year to establish the dramatic Belgian circuit as one of BMW's favorite battlegrounds. Many big names in the racing world campaigned this car, the championships were clocking up steadily, and the engines were giving in excess of 160 horsepower. Yet, on the circuits, the lightweight Alfa Romeos and Ford's Lotus Cortinas were beginning to get closer: BMW's response was to fit the newly developed 2-liter version of the M10, and the roadgoing 2000ti duly appeared early in 1966, paired with an extravagantly equipped "tilux" edition featuring executive-style interior appointments. In an early foretaste of today's automakers bragging about Nordschleife lap times, BMW boasted that the 2000ti was the "absolute fastest production car at the Nürburgring," with saloon car race ace Hubert Hahne having achieved an average speed of 137.2 kilometers per hour.

Even better performance was soon to come with the 2000tii, launched in late 1969. The extra "i" in the model's designation was of pivotal importance, for it signaled the arrival of fuel injection, something that had been mainly reserved for racing cars until that time. The Kugelfischer mechanical injection had indeed been used on racing versions, but it was adapted for road car use with the inclusion of an ingenious three-dimensional cam system that predated electronic control maps by regulating the fuel mixture according to a wide variety of parameters such as rpm, throttle opening, temperature, and air pressure.

A five-speed gearbox was again standard for the 2000tii, as was a substantial price premium over the regular carburetor-fed 2000ti. Quickly, the tii became a giant killer on the racetracks and big hit among automotive commentators, though its career was cut short in 1971 not just by the arrival of the new-look 5-Series but by another much smaller model, one destined to be one of the most important cars in the history of the company.

Small, Smart, and Spectacular: The 2002tii

The 2002tii arrived partly by accident and partly thanks to a series of happy coincidences. The so-called '02 series had been conceived in 1966 as a lower-cost entry point to the BMW range and was in effect a shortened "Neue Klasse" 1600 shorn of its rear passenger doors—hence the 1602 designation. Even with the meager 85 horsepower of the original 1.6-liter engine, it was light and fun to drive, ultimately becoming a huge and unexpected success, especially in the US. It was then

BMW hit the big time with the compact '02 series, especially in the United States. A particular highlight was the 2002tii with its revvy fuel-injection engine; it established a new benchmark for performance, handling, and small-car fun.

a matter of simple commercial and industrial logic to equip the '02 series with each successive engine upgrade received by its larger four-door parent, and by autumn 1968 it reached what then felt like its high point—the short-chassis '02 married to the 130-horsepower fuel-injected engine.

The tii—just these three letters are sufficient, the number is implicitly understood—proved to be a car that was vastly more than the sum of its pretty straightforward parts. The injection engine was brilliantly responsive, even from low rpm, and, with 130 horsepower on tap and barely a ton to motivate, it provided instantaneous and thrilling performance. Much like the Mini Cooper S of the 1960s or the Golf GTI later in the 1970s, the tii recalibrated everyone's expectations: it provided outrageous fun at an affordable price, pulling a whole generation of enthusiast buyers into BMW's orbit. It even tested the loyalty of wealthy Porsche, Jaguar, and Mercedes owners. On the racetracks it was the car to beat, too, with Dieter Quester taking numerous Touring Car championships in 1968 and 1969 and private drivers all over Europe scoring additional national titles in the years that followed.

Turbocharging: First and Fastest

The nucleus of highly talented racing department engineers around von Falkenhausen and Rosche had for some time been working in the background on competition developments of the 2-liter engine, experimenting with dual overhead camshafts and four valves per cylinder for Formula 2 and sports car applications. There were a great number of these, with over five hundred engines being supplied to customer teams and a multitude of well-known and soon-to-be-famous drivers achieving impressive results with their BMW power units. Yet, as BMW's own official account reveals, even von Falkenhausen's closest colleagues were left speechless

Straight from the track: the 1974 2002 Turbo used expertise gained in motorsport to produce the world's first volume-built turbocharged road car, but the sudden delivery of its 170 horsepower could catch drivers unawares.

The aggressive image of the 2002 Turbo shocked the commentators of the early 1970s, but ultimately it was killed off by the fuel crisis. With just 1,672 built, exclusivity is guaranteed.

when, on Christmas 1968, he announced his next project: "Let's try a turbocharger." Though some in-house technicians had been inclined to dismiss the challenge as a childish holiday season prank, the idea worked brilliantly. The output of the racing 2002 rose from 200 horsepower to 280 horsepower, and it won four rounds of the European Touring Car Championship in 1969 to secure a repeat title for BMW. Four years later, in a flurry of noise and excitement, the roadgoing 2002 Turbo arrived. Quite a bit of that noise was generated by its bold appearance, signaling a more aggressive approach than BMW customers were accustomed to. Fat, wide tires on broad rims were protected by bulging, riveted-on arches, just as on a racing car; a chunky black spoiler was attached to the trailing edge of the trunk lid; and a deep frontal air dam stretched perilously close to the ground. Worse, this air dam carried a full-width red, blue, and black color band with the legend "2002 turbo" superimposed in large white mirror script. The same message and stripes were repeated on the car's flanks. If ever there was a racer for the road, this was it.

Aggressive, for sure, and more especially so since visible aerodynamic aids like spoilers and splitters were almost never seen on road cars at the time. But BMW, for its part, could claim some justification for its exhibitionism: this was the first turbocharged car from a major manufacturer, predating the Porsche 911 Turbo by several months and the Saab 99 Turbo by several years. And its claimed performance was sensational for the time too: 170 horsepower when most 2-liters struggled to get past 125, with the 0–100 kilometer-per-hour sprint dispatched in much less than eight seconds and a top speed way beyond 200 kilometers per hour. Every aspiring racer wanted one, even at a price nearly double that of the car that had sired it, the highly acclaimed 2002tii. What could possibly go wrong?

Well, as has been extensively discussed in print, the Turbo was clearly a case of the right car at the wrong time. A global fuel crisis was probably the last thing on the minds of BMW Motorsport engineers around the turn of the decade as they set about developing the road car off the back of the racing program. Still less could they have anticipated the weekend driving bans and long lines at gas stations provoked by the Arab oil embargo. Europe was experiencing its first wave of anticar sentiment, and the Turbo's blatant message of unapologetic power and speed was unwelcome. As for the car itself, it was by turns thrilling and terrifying, a stimulating companion or a treacherous flatterer. It was exciting to drive—perhaps too exciting—and it soon earned the reputation of being a tricky customer.

The root cause was the engine rather than the chassis. In the absence of electronic controls for fueling and boost, BMW engineers had to specify low (6.9:1) compression pistons to avoid damaging preignition at higher revs when the turbo began to deliver boost. This made the car sluggish at low engine speeds, which encouraged the driver to press the throttle pedal harder to gain speed. However, after what seemed like an agonizing delay, the power would come in explosively and without warning, sending a huge burst of energy to break the grip of the rear tires despite the presence of a limited slip differential. In a straight line this could be exhilarating, but in the middle of a corner—especially in damp or slippery conditions—it could lead to a heart-stopping tail slide or even a spin.

Today, in the electronic 2020s, we are more accustomed to the surge of power that some turbo engines can deliver. Many commentators who now return to the 2002 Turbo with fresh eyes concede that it no longer seems so difficult to drive and that it may have been too harshly judged at the time. It's galling to realize that, had those 1970s BMW Motorsport engineers had the benefit of modern electronic engine management, traction control, and stability systems, the Turbo need not have been a handful at all.

Either way, BMW bowed to the inevitable, hurriedly deleting the mirror script on the Turbo's air dam, then hiking the car's price and, in the face of the continuing oil crisis, tapering production to zero by mid-1975. Just 1,672 examples were built over a stretch of little more than a year, all of them left-hand drive and built to European spec, with the overwhelming majority finished in white. By way of contrast, nearly 45,000 tiis found buyers, and the plain 2002 sold 326,000. In other words, as an exciting but glorious commercial failure as well as a signpost for the turbo era, this rarest of 2002s has all the right ingredients for lasting classic status.

Strictly speaking, the 2002 Turbo should be considered the first product of BMW's Motorsport division as it had been formally constituted in May 1972. It was an explosive enough start for the division, but even more controversy—and plenty more classics—were still to come.

1800 TiSA

Model name and code

1800 TiSA, Type 118

Claim to fame

Sensational first hit for BMW Motorsport: closest thing to a circuit-ready racer

Years in production

1964–1965

Number built

200

Launch price

DM 13,500 (€6,900)

Engine code and type

M10, straight four, SOHC 8-valve; twin Weber carburetors

Displacement, cc

1,773

Peak power hp @ rpm

130@6,100

Max torque, Nm @ rpm

157@5,250

Transmission and drive

5-speed manual, rear, limited slip differential

Suspension, front

MacPherson strut

Suspension, rear

Semi-trailing arms, coils

Body styles

4-door sedan

Curb weight, kg

1,050

Max speed (km/h) and 0–100 km/h (sec)

186; 9.0

Production by year

1964	200
Grand total	200

2002tii

Model name and code

2002tii, Type 114/E10

Claim to fame

Small, sophisticated, and fabulous fun; a breakthrough hit in the US

Years in production

1971–1975

Number built

44,484

Launch price

DM 10,990 (€5,620)

Engine code and type

M10, straight four, SOHC 8-valve; Kugelfischer fuel injection

Displacement, cc

1,990

Peak power hp @ rpm

130@5,800

Max torque, Nm @ rpm

176@4500

Transmission and drive

4-speed manual, rear

Alternative transmission

5-speed manual

Suspension, front

MacPherson struts

Suspension, rear

Semi-trailing arms, coils

Body styles

2-door sedan, 3-door Touring (hatch)

Curb weight, kg

990

Max speed (km/h) and 0–100 km/h (sec)

190; 9.4

Production by year

1975	1,330
1974	6,644
1973	11,606
1972	14,210
1971	10,694
Grand total	44,484

2002 Turbo

Model name and code

2002 Turbo, M114/E20

Claim to fame

First small Turbo: thrilling speed but tricky to drive; ahead of its time

Years in production

1974–1975

Number built

1,672

Launch price

DM 18,720 (€9,520)

Engine code and type

M10, straight four, SOHC 8-valve; Kugelfischer injection, KKK turbocharger

Displacement, cc

1,990

Peak power hp @ rpm

170@5,800

Max torque, Nm @ rpm

240@4,000

Transmission and drive

4-speed manual, rear, limited slip differential

Alternative transmission

Close-ratio 5-speed manual

Suspension, front

MacPherson strut

Suspension, rear

Semi-trailing arms, coils

Body styles

2-door sedan

Curb weight, kg

1,080

Max speed (km/h) and 0–100 km/h (sec)

211; 7.0

Production by year

1975	188
1974	1,477
1973	7
Grand total	1,672

For a key to specification tables, see page 221

FROM RACETRACK
TO ROAD

3

The heat of
competition
breeds brilliant
cars for BMW
customers

Legendary car, legendary
circuit. The big 3.0 CSL
Coupé thunders through
the spectacular high-speed
Eau Rouge kink at Spa
Francorchamps en route to
one of BMW's many victories
at the track.

▲ New-broom CEO Eberhard von Kuenheim (left) and new recruit Bob Lutz just before the 1973 BMW Supervisory Board meeting. Lutz was the man who hired Jochen Neerpasch with the explicit mission of winning on the racetracks.

▼ Lightweight materials used in the 1,200 specially built CSLs reduced the big Coupé racer's mass to 1,060 kilograms: Neerpasch's move turned the CSL into a formidable race winner and a multiple European Touring Car champion.

IT IS AUTUMN 1969 and Herbert Quant, BMW's guiding light and principal shareholder, has announced that a hitherto unknown forty-two-year-old, Eberhard von Kuenheim, is to take charge of the company the following year. Understandably, there is some consternation among senior managers. On the face of it, the company has been doing really well, with two successful model lines in the shape of the Neue Klasse and the '02 series, a turnover about to break the DM 1 billion barrier, and a healthy order book. And in development there is an exciting new model, the future 5-Series, and a brand-new plant in which to build it.

But for the ambitious incoming CEO that was not enough: he realized BMW needed to move higher and faster if it wanted to outgrow its regional roots. Managing director Gerhard Wilcke had just retired due to ill health and his high-profile sales director, Paul Hahnemann, a popular figure with BMW's dealers and its workforce, fully expected to be handed the role. Resentful at having been passed over for promotion, he and von Kuenheim reportedly clashed on several issues, leading to Hahnemann's departure soon afterward. This in turn cleared the way for the new CEO to hire fresh talent both from inside and outside the company—and one of his most decisive moves was to lure an ambitious sales manager away from Opel, the German arm of General Motors.

A tall, cosmopolitan Swiss-American with a keen aptitude for languages, Robert "Bob" Lutz would go on to lead Ford of Europe and, in the four decades that followed, all three of America's top automakers. Joining BMW as marketing director in 1971, he immediately set about taking control of the dealer network, especially the privately owned franchises in export markets that were making millions from their trade in BMWs. Lutz's other major move was to poach Ford's racing manager, Jochen Neerpasch, with the express intention of allowing BMW to exploit its racing activities as a marketing tool.

A Legend in Its Own Time: The 3.0 CSL

One of Neerpasch's conditions, as he later recalled, was that the motorsports operation be independent: "First of all, I asked for a separate company, not an internal department, like it was at Ford. Then, since I needed one thousand cars for a racing homologation, a problem I encountered at Ford, I asked for assurances that those one thousand cars shall be produced."

In May the following year, BMW Motorsport GmbH was formally established, with thirty-five employees on its payroll. Neerpasch was its director, with Chris Amon, Toine Hezemans, Hans-Joachim Stuck, and Dieter Quester signed as works race drivers along with Björn Waldegaard and Achim Warmbold on the rally team. Shortly afterward, engineer Martin Braungart also made the move from Ford; he was to play a key role in the development of the M1 supercar.

At their disposal was the potent 2002 (now weighing just 950 kilograms and with a 240 horsepower sixteen-valve engine under the hood) for rallies, while the much larger E9 coupé was available for circuit racing. The big 3.0 CSL (for Coupé Sport Leicht) had already been campaigned by external teams supported by BMW, such as Alpina and Schnitzer. Yet despite the impressive 360 horsepower on tap from its fuel-injected 3,340cc twelve-valve engine, the car as a whole had been struggling with excess weight compared with the ultralight but still powerful Ford Capris that, ironically, Neerpasch himself had helped create in his previous job.

"As we consider 1973 a year of development, we cannot count on winning this European Championship," he announced, while at the same time giving the go-ahead for an intense program to reduce the weight of the big coupé. His caution was unfounded, however, and BMW did scoop the overall championship: Hezemans was the top driver and BMW Motorsport GmbH's blue, purple, and red striped livery became a familiar sight among racing fans. This success kicked off a scarcely broken run of ten championships through to 1983, with the CSL followed by the 320i in 1980 and the 635CSi the year after.

The 3.0 CSL was the first big program delivered by the newly formed BMW Motorsport GmbH organization; the later M1 supercar was the first—and only—clean-sheet design not based on a production car. Design details from both models are regularly referenced in new BMW vehicles.

▲▲ *BMW Art Car Series: Frank Stella*
The dramatic, graph paper–themed CSL by Frank Stella was the second in BMW's Art Car series and was a crowd favorite when it competed in the 1976 24 Hours of Le Mans.

▲ The M10-based BMW engine dominated European Formula 2 racing for nearly a decade, again feeding back into road car engine design.

What linked all these race cars was the fact that they served as rolling laboratories for technical innovations that could later be applied to series production cars. With the 3.0 CSL, the initial emphasis had been on weight reduction, improved aero performance, and increased power, leading in its third and most extreme incarnation to the world-famous "Batmobile" homologation special. Technically available to the public at a price of DM 35,700, this ultimate CSL employed wild aerodynamic aids and brought together every materials development in BMW's repertoire to trim its weight down to around 1,060 kilograms. It continued to win on the racetracks long after BMW had withdrawn as an official works team, and it directly inspired the 635CSi that took BMW's winning streak beyond the middle of the decade.

On the engine front, the first twenty-four-valve units appeared on the race cars in 1973 with 430-plus horsepower; by the end of the decade some turbo versions were giving up to 800 horsepower. Another innovation to get its first trial on the racetracks was anti-lock braking, later to become standard equipment on the production 7-Series.

Frequent changes in the Touring Car racing rules meant BMW had to move with the times: the small 320i took the drivers' championship in 1980, while two years later the title was won in a works kit-equipped 528i sedan in an echo of the 1800 TiSA's successes in the mid-1960s. The 635CSi's official championship swan song came in 1986, crowning a highly successful year: already, the directly race-inspired twenty-four-valve M635CSi—M6 in the US—was on sale to the public, but waiting in the wings was something smaller, lighter, and ultimately even quicker and even more successful—the M3, which we will meet in chapter 5.

In-House Engine Expertise—and Formula 1

For a decade or more, BMW's preference for doing its engine development work in-house had kept its motorsports engineers busy and its works and customer teams on the winner's podium. But Touring Car circuit racing was not the only preoccupation of BMW Motorsport GmbH. Far from it, in fact, for several other highly ambitious programs had been underway in parallel for some time: the big coupés racing in US series, the Junior team fielding the 320i, and the M10-based engine, which dominated Formula 2 for ten years. Yet destined to be even bigger were a series of high-profile ventures that would propel BMW Motorsport into the very highest divisions of automobile racing and shape the brand's image in the eyes of every future generation of customers.

First, there was the glamorous M1 supercar (see chapter 4), and shortly afterward the ferociously powerful Formula 1 engine that sped Nelson Piquet to the World Champion's title in 1983. A decade later came the V-12 engine specially designed for McLaren's F1, the world's fastest road car and the only one to take overall victory in the 24 Hours of Le Mans. Add to these the triumph of BMW's own car at Le Mans in 1999 using that same engine, and the company's return to Formula 1 after the turn of the millennium—albeit with less conspicuous success—as both an engine builder and a factory team.

Even in the late 1960s there had been suggestions that BMW might go into Formula 1, but top management resisted buying into the idea. But by the late 1970s Renault had begun to campaign its 1.5-liter turbo V-6 cars against the standard three-liter opposition; the Renaults showed clear potential, despite their initial fragility, and BMW began to realize that it, too, might have a potential winner in the shape

BMW Art Car Series: Jenny Holzer
Perhaps the fastest of BMW's entire series of Art Cars is Jenny Holzer's treatment of the 1999 Le Mans–winning V-12 LMR. The open-cockpit racer's sleek white shape provided the ideal high-speed canvas for her slogan-based artistic style.

of its M10 engine. After all, the motor covered the 1.5- to 2.0-liter range and BMW Motorsport already had a wealth of experience with it—in Formula 2, in sports cars, and with turbocharging in Touring Car racing.

The Formula 1 program was officially announced in April 1980, causing some surprise for a variety of reasons, not least of which was that the race engine would be based on the existing M10, and that high-mileage used engine blocks taken from road cars might be employed. Masterminded by engine guru Paul Rosche, the 1.5-liter M12 was fitted with a sixteen-valve head topped by black cam covers with BMW M-Power cast into their upper faces. But in contrast to the compactness of the core engine, the big KKK turbocharger, the multiple manifolds, the heat exchangers, intercoolers, and all the complex heat shielding and pipework took up more space in the engine bay. Installed in the Brabham BT52, though, it still looked much simpler than the rival Renault and Ferrari V-6 units with their twin turbos.

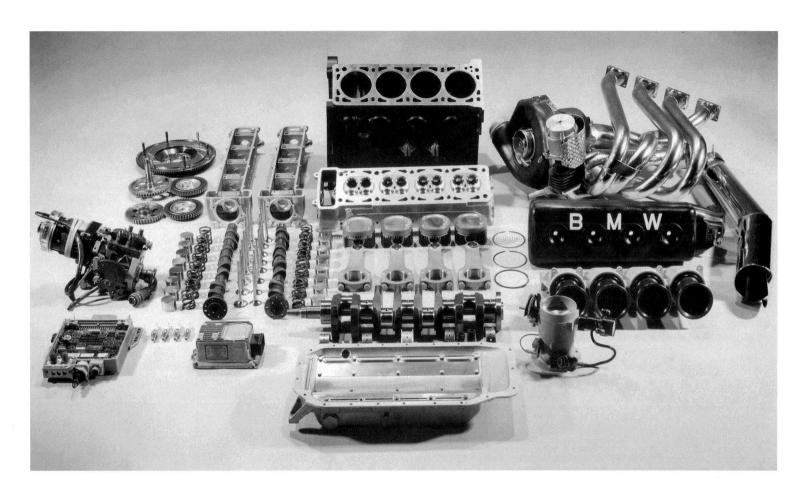

The initial engines, tested in secret throughout 1981, gave around 560 horse-power—more than enough to compensate for their extra weight compared with the 470 horsepower 3-liter Cosworth DFV V-8 that Brabham had been using. Even so, the car was difficult to drive; in 1982 Brabham didn't use the BMW engine on slower circuits. Despite the solitary 1–2, in Canada, reliability was patchy and blow-ups frequent—giving rise to the engine's nickname of "grenade." To everyone's dismay, these issues persisted until most of them were solved by new digital electronic mapping of the fueling and a clever fuel mix by BASF that prevented detonation under high boost pressures. That in turn opened the way to even more boost and the immense power levels that still enjoy pride of place in Formula 1 folklore.

"Suddenly the detonation was gone," recalled Rosche in a later interview. "We could increase the boost pressure, and the power, without problems. The maximum boost pressure we saw on the dyno was 5.6 bar absolute, at which the engine was developing more than 1,400 horsepower. It was maybe 1,420 or 1,450 horsepower, we really don't know because we couldn't measure it—our dyno only went up to 1,400."

"Maximum power was strictly for qualifying, though, only for one or two laps," he added. "In the race we ran about 1,000 horsepower. This was one of the reasons we won the championship in 1983."

Such is indeed the stuff of legends.

The most powerful engine in Formula 1 history, the 1.5 liter four-cylinder M12/13 was based on the roadgoing M10 but heavily turbocharged to produce upward of 1,400 horsepower in qualifying tune and 1,000 for the race itself. Reliability issues with early units were systematically ironed out by Paul Rosche's team to allow Nelson Piquet to clinch the 1983 World Driver's Championship.

McLaren chose BMW's 6-liter V-12 for its groundbreaking 1992 F1 supercar, and by 1995 the racing GTR version had swept to victory in the Le Mans 24 Hours—the first time a team had won the event at its first attempt.

BMW Powers McLaren to Le Mans Victory

Sadly, 1983 was destined to be the BMW Turbo's only truly successful year: over the seasons that followed, the wins were fewer and further apart. Nelson Piquet had defected to Williams-Honda, relations with Brabham owner Bernie Ecclestone were deteriorating, too, and the factory withdrew at the end of 1987 to concentrate on other ventures. One of these would involve Gordon Murray, the maverick Formula 1 design genius Rosche had clicked with so well at Brabham.

Murray had developed a lot of respect for Paul Rosche and had since moved to ultrasuccessful McLaren for the 1987 season. And it was against the background of this great success that a landmark conversation took place between McLaren team boss Ron Dennis and Murray, reportedly in an airport departure lounge as the two waited for their flight back home from a 1989 Grand Prix. Murray proposed that McLaren should build the ultimate road car, an uncompromised machine that would deliver a driving experience as close as possible to that of a Formula 1 car. To keep the car as compact as possible, Murray's concept would be a radical one: the driver would sit centrally for good visibility, with a passenger on either side. The structure would be fully carbon for lightness and strength, and no external aerodynamic aids would be permitted. His calculations suggested that a minimum of 600 horsepower was required to deliver the performance he wanted. As McLaren didn't have any engines, least of all a powerful engine for a road car, Murray was forced to look elsewhere.

At an early stage he had ruled out turbocharged engines because they did not provide the required response at low rpm. This made his task doubly challenging, but his insistence was understandable: this was the era of highly turbocharged 200-mile-per-hour supercars, such as the Ferrari F40, which were exhilarating but often tricky to drive smoothly. Murray's search eventually homed in on BMW and the 60-degree M70 V-12, as fitted in the 7-Series luxury sedan: this, he reasoned, could be further developed by BMW Motorsport to provide the required combination of power, flexibility, and low weight.

Though the Motorsport team under Rosche made extensive changes to the big engine, their task was made easier by the fact that they had previously developed an enhanced version of this V-12 for a prototype M8 edition of the E31 850CSi that was never put into production. This "M" V-12 had been enlarged to 6,064cc and fitted with dual overhead camshafts per bank and four valves per cylinder, giving 550 horsepower compared with the standard car's 380. This formed the basis for further development for the McLaren application, designated S70/2. Among the internal changes were a dry sump, a titanium crankshaft, and the use of magnesium instead of aluminum to save even more weight.

The installation in the compact engine bay of the F1 road car was complex, too, with four separate exhaust catalysts and a much-publicized gold leaf heat shield to keep temperatures under control. When the F1 was unveiled at the Monaco Grand Prix in May 1992, the results were truly sensational, with 636 horsepower giving a top speed of 390 kilometers per hour—still the highest of any nonturbo road car—and 0–100 kilometer-per-hour acceleration in 3.2 seconds.

McLaren initially ignored calls from customers for a racing version of the F1, but by 1995 the first GTR LM had appeared. The engine's rev limit and power were raised to 8,500 rpm and 680 horsepower, and straight-cut gears were fitted. The so-called "Famous Five" swept straight to a remarkable victory in that year's 24 Hours of Le Mans, finishing first, third, fourth, fifth, and thirteenth. This was the first time any team had won Le Mans in its debut year, and the first road car–based winner in many decades. Subsequent years saw new rules on inlet restrictors, which meant reducing the F1's power from the road car's standard 636 to 600 horsepower, but McLaren managed to shave 100 kilograms off the race cars' weight, and, with their improved aerodynamics, these even lighter cars continued to record better lap times.

Le Mans Win No. 2 Prompts a Formula 1 Comeback

The year 1995 would not be the only one in which BMW triumphed at Le Mans. Four years later, with the German company having switched its allegiance to Williams Grand Prix Engineering, the same V-12 engine in the back of the Williams-developed BMW Team Motorsport V-12 LMR prototype raced to victory ahead of a huge field of works teams that included Mercedes, Nissan, Toyota, and Audi. On BMW's first bid, in 1998, wheel bearing problems had forced the team to drop out early on in the French classic. But what was not so well known at the time of the 1999 triumph was that, back in 1997, the BMW board had given the green light to reenter Formula 1 in partnership with Williams, and that the 24-hour epic in France was in effect a trial run for the new Grand Prix venture.

BMW paired up with Williams Grand Prix Engineering in its own bid for Le Mans glory. Using the same engine as in the McLaren F1, the BMW Team Motorsport V-12 LMR prototype took top honors in the 1999 event.

Williams had already been testing BMW's new 3-liter V-10 E41/4 engine prior to its 2000 debut. It was an impressive start, with Ralf Schumacher scoring a podium in the team's first race, and the whole outfit finishing the season "best of the rest" behind the dominant Ferraris and McLaren-Mercedes. The following year, a new P80 engine brought 880 horsepower—reportedly the most powerful in the field—and four wins to again finish third in the Constructors' Championship. Fiery driving by Juan-Pablo Montoya resulted in seven pole positions and one win in 2003, to come a distant second in the Constructors' Championship to the all-conquering Ferrari; from then on, however, the team saw a series of diminishing returns despite huge investments of engineering and time under team boss Dr. Mario Theissen.

The engine, by now in its P84/85 incarnations, was giving upward of 950 horsepower at 19,800 rpm; it weighed just 82 kilograms, compared with the 117 kilograms of the original E41/4. A tribute to the skills—and deep pockets—of BMW Motorsport, it was best in class as far as power and reliability were concerned, but the results were still disappointing. This naturally led to impatience with Williams's performance on chassis development, and once again relationships became strained. BMW is understood to have tried to buy Williams out so as to gain complete control, but Sir Frank refused; this prompted the purchase in June 2005 of the Sauber team.

The fresh start in 2006, with another all-new engine—the P86—to comply with the new rules requiring 2.4-liter V-8s, brought a handful of podiums and a disappointing fifth in the Constructors' Championship despite the BMW Saubers often being third fastest behind the Ferraris and McLarens. In 2007, following McLaren's disqualification from the Constructors' title, BMW finished second, while the following year brought the team's only race win—in Canada—and another third overall. By now, however, the global financial crisis was in full swing, corporate budgets were

▲ The BMW Williams F1 team launch in 2004, from left to right: Patrick Head, drivers Juan-Pablo Montoya and Mark Gene, team boss Mario Theissen, Ralf Schumacher, and Sir Frank Williams.

◄ At the 2015 Sebring 12 Hours, BMW gave its Z4 GTLM contender (front) a fresh livery commemorating the 3.0 CSL's memorable victory at the Florida circuit forty years earlier.

being squeezed, and, rather than being helpful in promoting the brand, the hugely expensive Formula 1 program was delivering nothing but headaches. So to no one's surprise, the BMW board decided to throw in the towel in July 2009 and sell the team back to Peter Sauber.

Like many other big-league manufacturers, BMW had invested huge budgets in Formula 1, which had become vastly more competitive than it was two decades earlier when Piquet won the championship with BMW power. On the face of it, BMW Motorsport had little to show for its enormous multiyear racetrack campaign. Except, perhaps, that it did allow parent company BMW AG to stay true to its corporate mantra of bringing race car developments within reach of road car drivers. For, as we will see in chapter 7, the sensationally powerful third-generation M5 sedan, with its F1-inspired high-revving V-10 engine and seven-speed sequential transmission, did indeed bring Formula 1 technology to everyone's local BMW dealership.

BMW Art Car series: Alexander Calder
The first and perhaps the wildest of BMW's Art Cars was Alexander Calder's highly colorful 3.0 CSL of 1975. The New York sculptor, best known for his gently moving mobiles, was a friend of racing driver and art collector Hervé Poulain, who teamed up with Jochen Neerpasch to launch the series. Neerpasch can be seen back right in the photograph, in front of Calder's mobiles.

3.0 CSL

Model name and code	
3.0 CSL, E9	3.0 CSL (3.2), E9

Claim to fame	
Dramatic GT and ultra-successful light-weight race car; developed by Motor-sport division: the first real M car	The famous "Batmobile," the ultimate expression of Motorsport division's symbiosis between race and road

Years in production	
1971–1974	1973–1975

Number built	
1,208 (all versions)	

Launch price	
DM 35,700 (€18,250)	

Engine code and type	
M30, straight six, SOHC 12-valve, twin Zenith carburettors	M30, straight six, SOHC 12-valve; Bosch D-Jetronic fuel injection

Displacement, cc	
2,985	3,153

Peak power hp @ rpm	
180@6,000	206@5,600

Max torque, Nm @ rpm	
255@3,700	286@4,200

Transmission and drive	
Getrag 4-speed manual, rear, 25% limited slip differential	Getrag 4-speed manual, rear, 25% limited slip differential

Suspension, front	
MacPherson struts, Bilstein gas dampers	MacPherson struts, Bilstein gas dampers

Suspension, rear	
Semi-trailing arms, coils	Semi-trailing arms, coils

Body styles	
Two-door coupé	Two-door coupé

Curb weight, kg	
1,200	1,250

Max speed (km/h) and 1–100 km/h (sec)	
215; 7.3	220; 7.1

Production by year (all models)	
1975	17
1974	40
1973	438
1972	601
Grand total	1,096

McLaren F1

Model name and code
McLaren F1, F1

Claim to fame
BMW-M V-12 made the F1 the world's fastest road car and first to win Le Mans

Years in production
1992–1997

Number built
100

Launch price
£630,000 (€760,000)

Engine code and type
S70/2, 60-degree V-12, DOHC, 48-valve; Bosch electronic fuel injection

Displacement, cc
6,064

Peak power hp @ rpm
636@7,500

Max torque, Nm @ rpm
617@4,000

Transmission and drive
6-speed manual, rear

Suspension, front
Double wishbones, coils

Suspension, rear
Double wishbones, coils

Body styles
Mid-engined 3-seater coupé

Curb weight, kg
1,140

Max speed (km/h) and 1–100 km/h (sec)
390; 3.2

For a key to specification tables, see page 221

M1: THE
ELEGANT
INSPIRATION

4

The BMW supercar that became an icon—and how it nearly didn't make it into production

The M1 found fame not only as an elegant design but also as a high-speed work of art. Andy Warhol's colorful hand-painted example, the fourth in BMW's now-famous series of Art Cars, took part in the 1979 Le Mans 24 Hours and finished second in its class.

The exquisite proportions of the M1 still appear fresh and modern forty years down the line, and the design is regarded as one of Giorgietto Giugiaro's finest.

TODAY, THE M1 IS REVERED as one of the most precious crown jewels in BMW's treasure cabinet, enjoying quasi-iconic status among fans and collectors alike. Yet by any rational yardstick the endeavor was never much short of disastrous throughout its protracted gestation, and most companies would have canceled the program long before it sank even deeper into the financial mire.

But BMW top brass, to their great credit, bravely decided to stick with it, and the skillful turnaround engineered by quick-thinking image-makers helped transform a looming commercial disaster into a magical PR triumph. Indeed, before the wider public had become the wiser, the project had been repackaged as a great success and the M1 itself went on to become one of the German brand's most enduring and influential halo models.

Unquestionably, the M1 still serves as a central inspiration for all the generations of highly profitable M Cars that it sired, albeit indirectly. It's not for nothing that M Division's current chief designer, Marcus Syring, reveals that to this day nearly every designer in the studio still aspires to draw a worthy successor to this forty-year-old supercar, a design widely regarded as one of the most perfect automotive shapes ever created.

Yet even in this fulsome praise is an irony in the fact that the M1 was something of an evolutionary dead end in every respect, bar its remarkable twenty-four-valve, M88 inline six-cylinder engine. The fabulously exotic, low-slung Giorgietto Giugiaro body style picked up on the design cues of Paul Bracq's groundbreaking Turbo concept of 1972, but it was not followed up until the reverential Hommage concept car three decades later. Likewise, the mid-engined coupé architecture found no echo in a production car until the ambitious i8 plug-in hybrid in 2013. On a technical level, the M1's use of fiberglass as a body material was never repeated, and the pedigree race-specification suspension and running gear also remained a one-off.

Racetrack Targets: Ferrari and Porsche

The origins of the M1 project, codename E26, date back to the mid-1970s. Though BMW's big 3-liter, six-cylinder CSL coupés were at the peak of their winning form in the European Touring Car Championship, the model had already been replaced in the showrooms by the 635 series, and it was clear that a new top-level competition car was needed in order to boost the firm's international profile.

The recently founded BMW Motorsport GmbH division under Jochen Neerpasch (and, indirectly, Bob Lutz) decided to aim high, commissioning a mid-engined coupé to compete against Porsches and Ferraris in international Group 5 racing for so-called special production cars. This series effectively required a minimum homologation production run of four hundred cars over a twenty-four-month period. The idea, Jochen Neerpasch said later, was to build a race car and then convert it into a road car. "We wanted to price the road car at 100,000 DM and the racing version at 150,000 DM, when our racing 3.0 CSL cost 350,000 DM. We also wanted Paul Rosche [BMW engine expert] to develop a new 3.0-liter V-8 that could also be used in a Formula 1 car."

The V-8 never materialized, perhaps because BMW already had its excellent in-house M90 straight six, but for everything else BMW had to shop elsewhere. Italy's Lamborghini, riding high on the success of its groundbreaking Miura supercar, was commissioned to design and build the spaceframe chassis. Designer Giorgietto Giugiaro, whose star was also in the ascendant following the launch of the VW Golf and Lotus Esprit, took on the shaping of the fiberglass body, and other top-level suppliers such as ZF provided the race-standard transmission, limited slip differential, and other chassis components.

▲▲ The M1's interior looks stark and functional to today's eyes, but in the late 1970s it was well received. Best of all, everything worked effectively and reliably. The five-speed gearchange had a dogleg first gear, to the left and backward.

▲ The twin BMW roundels on the rear corners were Giugiaro's neat solution to giving the M1 a clear brand identity.

With Martin Braungart coordinating the project's many players, Neerpasch recalls that it was a "fantastic" technical cooperation. "At least once a week in 1977, taking turns, Martin and I would drive from Garching to [Lamborghini HQ] Sant'Agata getting faster and faster as we improved the car, each trying to beat the other's time. In the end we cut 30 minutes from our time."

Before long, as has been well documented, Lamborghini struck cashflow problems. Its request to BMW for a bailout loan was refused and all prototypes, stock, parts, and equipment connected with the M1 were swiftly scooped up by night and returned to Germany.

The BMW board did briefly discuss buying Lamborghini, but instead decided to entrust Giugiaro with organizing the assembly of the chassis and body using local

Italian specialists, which even included a group of ex-Lamborghini engineers. Longstanding Stuttgart coachbuilder Baur took on final assembly, including the installation of the BMW engine. By now, Paul Rosche had come up with a further improved twin-cam twenty-four-valve cylinder head for the M90, derived from the racing CSL's and incorporating mechanical fuel injection and separate throttle bodies for each cylinder—something that would become a signature feature on many successive generations of M engines. The new dry-sumped engine, now coded M88, would, said Rosche, be capable of 277 horsepower in road trim, 470 for Group 4 racing, and up to 850 or even 1,000 horsepower for Group 5. The chassis was designed to handle all of these power outputs.

The upshot of all this disruption was that the E26 program fell hopelessly behind schedule, a time line that had called for the four hundred production vehicles to be completed by spring 1978. The blow was twofold. Not only were customers for the road car becoming impatient and canceling their orders but, more seriously, the ever-shifting world of motorsport regulations had moved on and the Group 5 "silhouette" category for which the M1 was designed was set to disappear before the car was even ready.

This posed an existential threat to the whole M1 program, yet the ever-resourceful Neerpasch and Max Mosely, in charge of Formula 1 at the time, were able to come up with an ingenious answer—reputedly over several gin and tonics in a Munich bar. Their idea of a high-profile, one-make racing series on Formula 1 weekends, with Grand Prix drivers competing against privateers, all in identical BMW M1s, quickly gained traction and became part of the FIA Motorsport calendar for the 1979 season. The Procar series, although it only lasted two seasons, certainly lived up to its promise, with lots of spectacular on-track action and some epic battles between seasoned Grand Prix veterans such as Niki Lauda (champion in 1979), Nelson Piquet (the 1980 champion), and leading GT and Touring Car drivers. Generous prizes certainly helped, and few people cared that some perhaps even quicker pilots from teams like Ferrari had been forbidden to take part for commercial reasons.

1979: An M1 in the Procar pits with Martin Braungart (left), Jochen Neerpasch (center), and reigning F1 world champion Mario Andretti, only the second American to take the top title.

▲ A densely packed field of M1s charges into the first corner at the start of the 1979 Procar race on the Zolder circuit. Drivers included Grand Prix professionals and private entrants.

◄ Forty years on: an M1 racecar in the M1 Procar Revival at the Norisring, July 2019.

"I love that car. It has turned out better than the artwork."
-Andy Warhol

▲ Andy Warhol at work on his M1 Art Car in 1979. His vivid brush-painted color technique combined remarkably well with the finely drawn lines of Giugiaro's bodywork to produce a memorable race car.

◥ Jochen Neerpasch watches an M1 Procar cross the finishing line at the 2019 Procar revival at the Norisring.

For BMW the glamorous world of Formula 1 had done what the doctor ordered. The M1 showed off its strikingly good looks to maximum effect and to a worldwide audience, even if some of the cars ended their races with visible battle scars. Big motorsports names became associated with the car and, most critically, customer orders for road-ready M1s began to come in—even though the BMW's six-cylinder engine offering was seen by some as modest in comparison with the mighty V-8s and V-12s fielded by the company's Italian rivals.

◄ As a road car, the M1 is surprisingly benign and forgiving, but the powerful scream of its twenty-four-valve engine is unforgettable.

▼ 1979: Group 4 M1 at full speed, clearly showing the broad rear spoiler and extended wheelarches of the racing version. In contrast to most other supercars, the M1 was designed first and foremost as a racing car, but one that would be well suited to road use too.

One of the most familiar shots of the roadgoing M1, showing its elegant proportions and perfect detailing to maximum effect. The shimmering wheels are a particular highlight.

Race Car Turns Road Car

But what of the M1 as a road car? To anyone brought up with the extravagant supercars of the 2020s, the M1 comes across as beautifully low, pure, and compact—and of course still highly attractive. It is a design that has worn its forty years extremely well: its proportions and stance on the road are nigh-on perfect and many of its exquisite details, such as the slatted rear-window cover, the twin BMW roundels at the rear, and the stunning, shimmering wheels have gone on to acquire a timeless quality of their own.

By contrast, in most respects the M1's engineering is worlds apart from today's super-complex, computer-controlled machinery. The 3.5-liter twin-cam straight six, with its beautifully black-finished cam covers, sits in a midships engine bay that could clearly accommodate a much larger eight- or even twelve-cylinder unit. The dogleg-shift five-speed ZF transaxle is there in full view, unencumbered by radiators, intercoolers, or other trunking, and the racing-style double wishbone suspension relies on standard steel springs and Bilstein adjustable shocks all round. The rack-and-pinion steering is unassisted.

The chassis was designed at Lamborghini by GianPaolo Dallara, who went on to found his own very successful racing car manufacturing business. Constructed of square-section steel tubing, the chassis was in line with racing practice at the time. Ready for the road, the M1 weighs an impressive 1,300 kilograms; with the standard engine giving 277 horsepower at 6,500 rpm, the car feels quick, agile, and responsive. Most of all, it comes across as beautifully well balanced and with a generous spread of power from its nonturbo engine.

By today's standards the two-seater cabin is sparse and monotone in nature, but it was perfectly acceptable in its day; a Ferrari F40, for example, is even more utilitarian. Standard equipment on road versions included air conditioning, audio system, and power windows, and the only trim color option was black. Of the five exterior color options, by far the most popular choice was white, followed by orange, red, and a very stylish dark blue.

Just 399 roadgoing M1s were built over the model's two-year production period, while the tally of racing versions, including those for the Procar series, amounted to fifty-four. BMW had undoubtedly burned its fingers with the venture: by late 1980 top management wanted rid of the project as soon as possible, even though some prominent figures—most notably Jochen Neerpasch, the father figure of BMW Motorsport GmbH—argued that, properly developed, the M1 could have done for BMW what the 911 did for Porsche.

Contemporary road tests were full of admiration for the M1's benign nature, with *Motor Sport*'s Jeremy Walton even deliberately taking his example out on snow-covered roads in Germany:

> The exciting part of this supercar is that it is just as drivable as many less exotic saloons. Whereas some exotics seem to be cumbersome when you get them onto a B-road, or challenge them with wildly changing surfaces and cambers, the M1 is at its best. I felt so happy with it, that I would let the rear wheels power out of line in second or third under full power, because the chassis took care of me. The steering could be gently turned into the direction of the skid, and the M1 would track obediently into line with none of the snap, or heart-in-mouth feel that some more established supercars engender.
>
> [The M1] is a superb road vehicle, worthy of a commercial future as a flagship and a supremely capable performer. It is, above all, a practical everyday machine, not a Stratos-style homologation special. BMW insisted on their normal levels of fit and finish. We have yet to encounter, or read a report, by anyone who did not think the M1 was a true super car.

▶▶ BMW Classic's own M1 poses in front of the i8—two exotic mid-engined coupés that stand out as landmark designs but that share very little in terms of their engineering and construction.

Driving the M1 for the first time in 2020, seasoned journalist Peter Robinson praised the flexibility and "never less than glorious" sound of the six-cylinder engine, but echoed the age-old criticisms of the heavy, long-travel clutch and weighty steering at low speeds. "No, it doesn't feel supercar-quick," wrote Robinson, "but it's eager and responsive. . . . Its composure and stability are staggering; by today's standards the modest tires mean grip levels are less than heroic, but the advantage is the kind of involvement that too many modern supercars lack."

Out of Character—but Great for BMW

Just like the 507 a quarter century before it, the M1 is universally celebrated in the BMW world. It is very special and very rare, and the few examples that come up for auction command eye-watering prices. But does it represent the best of BMW? Perhaps not. Indeed, it is probably the most un-BMW-like BMW ever built, a sudden departure from the company's core values of doing as much as possible in-house and under continuous hands-on quality control. It could also be seen as a vanity project that was a clear departure from CEO Eberhard von Kuenheim's successful strategy of steady and well-planned expansion based on firm foundations.

BMW was certainly unlucky that its heat-of-the-moment tactic of entrusting key tasks to outside companies backfired so badly: the mix-ups and resultant delays cost the German firm a fortune, said by some to be the equivalent of a whole year's Formula 1 budget. On the face of it, it didn't lead anywhere useful, at least not in the short term. But while the M1 can justifiably be seen to have failed both as a motorsport venture and a commercial project, its equally justifiable successes as a design and as a driving machine have assured it a prominent place in automotive history. Cars designed for racing rarely make satisfactory road cars, but BMW's exceptional expertise, even in the late 1970s, helped make the M1 a powerful exception to this maxim.

What is perhaps more powerful still is the lesson BMW learned from this never-to-be repeated gamble, something that has held BMW Motorsport GmbH and then M GmbH in good stead ever since: treat one-off projects and freestanding halo ventures with caution, and continue to develop exciting high-performance M Cars from regular series-production models where they not only benefit from maximum economies of scale but also sprinkle their magic dust over the directly related cars that people can actually buy.

Time is the great healer, and while the experience of the M1 was a bitter and costly one at the time, this oft-criticized project did more than just leave us with a fabulous car admired by all. In the more important bigger picture, the M1 also taught BMW's Motorsport division some painful lessons, lessons that were swiftly adopted and which soon allowed an agile BMW to snatch a head start over all other automakers and produce true high-performance road cars idolized by enthusiast buyers the world over.

M1

Model name and code	
M1, E26	
Claim to fame	
Audacious supercar venture that started it all	
Years in production	
1978–1981	
Number built	
399 road cars, 54 race cars	
Launch price	
DM 100,000 (€51,100)	
Engine code and type	
S88, straight six, DOHC 24-valve	
Displacement, cc	
3,453	
Peak power hp @ rpm	
277@6,500	
Max torque, Nm @ rpm	
330@5,000	
Transmission and drive	
5-speed ZF transaxle, rear, 40% limited slip differential	
Suspension, front	
Double wishbones, coil springs, gas dampers	
Suspension, rear	
Double wishbones, coil springs, gas dampers	
Body styles	
Two-door mid-engined coupé	
Curb weight, kg	
1,300	
Max speed (km/h) and 1–100 km/h (sec)	
250; 6.5	
Production by year	
1981	55
1980	251
1979	115
1978	29
Grand total	450

For a key to specification tables, see page 221

THE 1980s

M3, M5, M6—
THE GEN-1 FAVORITES

5

First-generation M-Division customer cars deliver dazzling performance

The first M3 hit the market two years after BMW Motorsport had launched the M5 and M635CSi, but its impact and influence were vastly bigger. An energetic and agile racer for the road, it has served as the inspiration for every M-Car since.

▼ Heart of the matter: the M88/3 straight six from the M1 employed four valves per cylinder for a power output of 286 horsepower, putting the M635CSi in a league of its own when it came to performance, tractability, and, especially, a glorious soundtrack when opened up in anger.

▼▼ Elegant and understated but supremely potent, the first-ever series-production M-Car was the M635CSi in 1984. Known as the M6 in the US, it fused the timeless grace of the Paul Bracq-styled 6-Series Coupé with the race-bred 24-valve straight six direct from the M1 supercar. As with all its successors, its high price reflected its sophisticated engineering content and appointments.

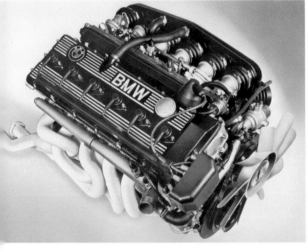

WITH ITS CLICHÉD IMAGES of big hair, extravagant power dressing, and a winner-take-all competitive culture, the decade of the 1980s is often regarded as one of lax regulation, fat salaries, and unbridled entrepreneurial excess. For its part, BMW steered clear of the worst of the stock market hysteria, but it was certainly a willing accomplice when it came to helping the new wave of Champagne-swilling young executives spend their inflated bonuses. The prestige and the powerful, sharp-handling image of the 3- and 5-Series models were perfectly aligned with the aggressive city types of the era; the slightly rebellious streak embodied in a BMW made it the ideal foil with which the nouveau riche could taunt their stuffy elders in their staid Mercedes and Jaguars.

Helping fuel that image had been the highly visible M1 supercar—never mind that it had been a commercial disaster—and, on a more limited level, the Formula 1 World Championship in 1983, with the most powerful engine ever seen on a racetrack. Yet for committed high-performance enthusiasts—even those with a healthy bank balance—BMW could offer precious little fast or furious enough to tempt them: it had been nearly a decade since the heyday of the 2002tii, the Turbo, and the big six-cylinder E9 coupés, and the elegant Bracq-styled 6-Series flagship launched in 1976 was proving more of a grand touring coupé than a sports machine to set the pulses racing.

Elegance Incarnate: M635CSi, the First M Car for the Road

Fortunately, BMW didn't keep those potential customers waiting too long, even though the M635CSi unveiled at the 1983 Frankfurt Motor Show did its best to avoid proclaiming its much-anticipated high-performance specification. So sober and elegant was its demeanor that few would have guessed that under the hood beat the six-cylinder, twenty-four-valve heart of the exotic M1 sports car. Indeed, with only a deeper front air dam and fractionally wider forged aluminum wheels, there was little clue that this was a machine of truly exceptional speed and power. A clearly logical engineering and commercial move on BMW's part, the M635CSi (which would be redesignated M6 for the US and Japanese markets) was precisely

what everyone had been waiting for. And, just like the 2002tii of the 1970s, it helped establish a template for future M Cars that has been consistently successful for half a century since: a highly engineered, state-of-the-art engine and driveline delivering scintillating performance, allied to a substantially upgraded chassis, steering, and brakes—but with precious few external changes to advertise the fact.

For the engineers, creating the M635CSi had been a relatively straightforward task, as the standard car was already highly specified. The M1's M88 twenty-four-valve engine slotted straight in. The only big changes were the move to a baffled wet sump, different pistons and connecting rods, and the addition of Bosch's sophisticated Motronic engine management system to help improve efficiency and increase power fractionally to 286 horsepower at 6,500 rpm. That was a substantial output for a car that weighed little more than 1,500 kilograms. It was fed through a five-speed Getrag manual gearbox to the rear axle fitted with a 25 percent limited slip differential. Chassis upgrades included stiffer springs and Bilstein shocks all around, along with heavier anti-roll bars and larger 300mm ventilated discs at the front. M6-badged versions fitted with catalytic converters for the US and Japanese market had the subtly different S38 engine, with milder cams, lower compression, and 30 horsepower less. The chassis kept the standard ride height too.

As evidence of their thoroughness in pursuing perfectly balanced handling, the Motorsport engineers quickened the recirculating ball steering and then moved the battery to the trunk to ensure optimal weight distribution. The only changes to the interior were a speedometer reading up to 280 kilometers per hour—not far beyond the CSi's top speed—and a subtle M logo set into the rev counter. Performance was, unsurprisingly, pretty sensational, with 100 kilometers per hour available in 6.4 seconds from standstill—a figure that's still respectable today. Similarly, the quoted

Successive generations of big BMW coupés have struggled to match the classy style of the original M635CSi/M6.

▲ The M635CSi was quickly pressed into Touring Car racing programs as the spiritual successor to the legendary 3.0 CSL. Its racing career lasted until late into the 1980s.

◤ Dressed up for the 1980s: the first M535i, based on the E12 5-Series, was not a proper M-Car but a body-kit exercise using the regular 3.5-liter engine.

▼ False start: despite its M-badged grille, frontal air dam, and side sill moldings, the 1985 M535i only carried the standard 218 horsepower engine and was more of a styling exercise than a genuine M Car.

top speed of 255 kilometers per hour made the CSi one of the fastest four-seaters of its day. The chassis changes were skillfully judged to deal with the additional power and loadings that the big coupé was likely to experience, but in no way did they impinge on its status as a supremely fast and comfortable cross-continent express. The fabulous racetrack sound of the straight six accelerating hard to its red line was perhaps the only real indulgence conceded by the Motorsport engineers, again setting a trend for future generations of M Cars.

Where there was criticism, however, was around the substantial price charged for the new car: at almost DM 90,000 when launched (equivalent to $87,000 today), it was pegged at nearly double the entry-level model in the 6-Series line. Not that this proved much of a deterrent to buyers: close on 5,500 were sold over the CSi's five-year production lifetime, during which the car remained exclusive and appealing, and hardly changed at all. Indeed, high purchase prices have been a feature of BMW M models ever since, and the sky-high reputation of this, the first proper M Car, makes it one of the most desirable among enthusiasts and collectors.

E28 M535i: A False Start

It's not often that BMW gets spooked by another car manufacturer, let alone its longest-running and closest adversary. But this is just what happened in the autumn of 1983 when Mercedes-Benz surprised the auto industry by unveiling its 190E 2.3-16. The habitually staid and stuffy Stuttgart brand had launched its compact 190 series the year before, entering the middle market territory of BMW's 3-Series; perhaps to BMW's relief, the newcomer had proved as dull to drive as its bigger brothers. But the revelation that Mercedes had gone to Cosworth in the UK, builders of the world's most successful Formula 1 engines, for a high-performance 190 derivative came as a big shock to the system—especially as the 2.3-16 boasted a full 185 horsepower in roadgoing trim and was clearly a homologation model with its eye on the new DTM German Touring Car championships due to start the next year. BMW's second-generation 3-Series, the E30, was already selling well and there was a high-performance derivative under development, set for release in 1986. But that was not soon enough to counter the threat from the Mercedes Cosworth: perhaps as a panic reaction, the company rush-released a sportier version of the 5-Series, the M535i. This was one of only a few M models to disappoint commentators: despite sharing the M prefix and a 3.5-liter engine displacement with the exotic 6-Series coupé, the M535i was more of a cosmetic exercise than a genuine Motorsport engineering development.

The engine was the standard single-cam, twelve-valve M30 from the regular 5-Series and gave 218 horsepower; the optional close-ratio gearbox and automatic transmission were already on the options list for the standard car, as were the M-Technic suspension and alloy wheels. The main difference was an extensive body kit, which did little for the aerodynamics but accentuated the heavy look of the car. On the positive side, it was reasonably well priced at DM 50,000 and went on to sell 45,000 units in the four years it remained in production.

E28: The First M5 Packs Exhilaration with Discretion

Fortunately, it was only a matter of months before those negative reactions turned sharply positive: the M5, unveiled at the Amsterdam show early in 1985, was as brilliant as the M535i was disappointing. Its exterior, much more sober than the flashy M535i, was barely distinguishable from that of a standard 5-Series, the only giveaways being a modest frontal air dam below the bumper, specific M alloy wheels, and discreet M5 badges on the grille and trunk lid. Inside, as with the M653CSi/M6, only a 280-kilometer-per-hour speedometer, a rev counter with an inset M logo, a three-spoke M-Technic steering wheel, and an M-branded gear lever knob set the M5 apart from lesser 5-Series models.

Again, as the big coupé had so elegantly proved, it was what lay below the largely unchanged skin that really mattered. The biggest attraction, and the one everyone had been waiting for, was the mighty twenty-four-valve six-cylinder M88 engine, rated at 286 horsepower at 6,500 rpm, straight out of the exotic M1 and identical to that in the M635CSi. This was paired with a Getrag five-speed manual transmission and a 25 percent limited slip differential on the rear axle. Upgrades to the suspension, braking, and steering paralleled those of the coupé.

Under the radar: launched in 1985, the first "real" M5 was intentionally plain-looking on the outside but carried the M1's potent 24-valve six underneath. Its prodigious performance combined with luxurious comfort and docile driving characteristics to create an entirely new class of car.

▲ The badge that means so much. Ever since the 1985 original, the M5 nameplate has stood for supercar performance allied to discreet and sober styling and first-class comfort for four.

▼ The E30 M3 was unashamedly a racing car from the outset and dominated the Touring Car racing scene into the 1990s, making it the most successful racer in BMW's history.

In contrast to the M535i, which was built on BMW's volume production line at Dingolfing, all M5s were virtually hand-built by Motorsport employees, initially at the Preussenstrasse site and later at Garching after BMW Motorsport GmbH had moved its headquarters there. Perhaps reflecting this specialist labor content, the M5 launched at a price of DM 80,750, about a 50 percent increase from the cost of the lesser M535i.

Once again, there was criticism of the high price, but this was silenced as soon as it was realized that the M5 was something truly special, something with a combination of qualities that had never been seen before. On one hand it was beautifully refined, easy and gentle to drive around town and wherever discretion was demanded; in that sense it was as silky sweet as any other six-cylinder 5-Series, and even the ride comfort was good. But on the open road, the highway, or even the racetrack, it was able to unleash an altogether more sensational side, with searing acceleration through the gears right round to the exhilarating 7,000 rpm red line. Its poise on the road was excellent, too, thanks to the uprated chassis.

Taken as a whole, this was a Porsche level of performance, but with the ability to carry four adults in comfort. These remarkable attributes made it unique in the market and set the tone for all M5s to come: impeccably engineered, beautifully equipped, and discreet in appearance—but devastatingly fast whenever the need should arise.

E30 M3: Racer for the Road Causes a Sensation

As far as BMW Motorsport GmbH was concerned, the E30 M3 was the big one, the big breakthrough. For though the first M3 was smaller in size than the M5 and M635CSi that preceded it to market, it was much bigger in its impact, its influence, and its sales volume: almost eighteen thousand were built between the original launch in 1986 and when the last cabriolet version left the production line in 1991.

The most important difference of all was in Motorsport's approach with the car: rather than starting with a civilized sedan and then enhancing it for superior performance on the public road, the M3 was unashamedly a racing car from the very outset, targeted at winning races, and only slightly tamed for road use by regular customers. The targets in question were the DTM German championship and Touring Car championships all over the world, and this required an initial homologation batch of five thousand examples to be built and sold. For this reason, the M3's assembly took place at BMW's main Milbertshofen plant, the drivetrain having been built by special teams on a side line.

Given BMW's wealth of experience with the four-cylinder M10 engine and its sixteen-valve derivatives in competition, the choice of powerplant for the M3 was straightforward. The bore and stroke were stretched to provide a displacement of 2,302cc, and early prototype engines even employed cutdown versions of the M88's twenty-four-valve head. Initial power outputs of the S14 unit were encouraging, at 200 horsepower at 6,750 rpm in noncatalyst form. Early exhaust aftertreatment systems sapped some of that power, but later versions with improved digital fuel injection and electronics provided equal outputs to noncatalyst models.

The modifications that turned the standard E30 3-Series into the M3 were more extensive than the model's low-key exterior would suggest. The clearest identifiers are the swollen wheelarches, the sill moldings, and the raised rear deckline carrying a substantial spoiler.

▲ ▶▶ Production M3s for regular customers were only slightly tamed for street use, and regular Evolution upgrades for racing made for ever more thrilling driving experiences on the road. The ultimate Sport Evo development of the engine, identifiable by its red plug leads, saw the 16-valve unit taken out to 2.5 liters and 238 horsepower.

▶ Convertible versions helped broaden the M3's appeal beyond its original hardcore sports clientele.

For the European market, a close-ratio five-speed gearbox with a dogleg first gear was fitted, while the US and Japan had a conventional H-pattern overdrive five-speed. Both had a 25 percent limited slip differential. The standard suspension was extensively revised, with shorter and stiffer springs, repositioned anti-roll bars, special shocks, and, on the front, a lot more steering caster. The steering rack was quickened, the tracks widened, and the brake discs enlarged to 280mm vented at the front and 282mm solid at the rear. The standard tire fitment was 205/55 on 15-inch cross-spoke alloy wheels; later, 16-inch wheels would come into play.

On the exterior, almost everything changed. Smoothly flared quattro-style wheel-arches housed the wider wheels and tires, the front and rear panels were subtly altered to benefit airflow and cooling, and the trunk lid was raised and the rear window re-angled in order to improve the overall aerodynamics. Changes to the interior were limited to sports seats, a rear seat shaped for two passengers, and an oil temperature gauge in place of the econometer inset in the rev counter. Some limited series models carried a numbering plaque on the dashboard.

Ready for the road, the M3 weighed some 1,200 kilograms. This low mass, allied to the near-200 horsepower engine output, gave intoxicating performance. BMW's claimed 6.7 seconds to 100 kilometers per hour was undercut as soon as magazines completed their first tests, and the response from commentators was one of almost universal praise. "It is virtually a racing car which can comfortably be driven on the road," wrote Gordon Cruickshank in *Motor Sport*, "and there are not many of those available."

But what was even more impressive than the numbers delivered by the early M3 was the *way* it performed. Here was a raw and ready racer, eager to rocket away at the slightest opportunity: the merest brush of the throttle would send it urgently

leaping ahead, and the firm ride and quick steering combined to give it an almost hyperactive, race car responsiveness and sense of engagement. It was hard to imagine a bigger contrast to the svelte, super-sophisticated M5 that the BMW Motorsport GmbH engineers had signed off just a year before, and many saw this as evidence of the division's remarkable breadth of skills. If there were any minuses on those first M3s, they were the notchy gear change (first gear being back and to the left), the noise at cruising speeds, and, for Brits at least, the fact that all M3s were left-hand drive only.

BMW may have had little idea at the time that it was unleashing such a phenomenon, one that would turn into a horsepower arms race and come to dominate the high-performance car scene for three decades. Initial Touring Car rules had stipulated five thousand road car sales to gain homologation for Group A racing. Now, an extension of those rules also allowed "Evolution" components to be fitted to race cars, provided more than five hundred road cars had been sold with those parts. Thus, the M3, in tandem with its racetrack rivals, went through a series of almost yearly upgrades, all of which were reflected in roadgoing limited-edition Evolution models of steadily increasing power and performance. These culminated in the 2.5-liter, 7,000 rpm, 238 horsepower Sport Evolution of early 1990.

This was the clearest example, yet again, of BMW's core philosophy in action—exploiting racetrack experience for the direct benefit of BMW enthusiasts on the public road. In the case of the M3, it led to some truly unforgettable models—and arguments still rage about which of the many variants and special editions are the purest and most exciting expression of the M3 ethos. There is already a serious collectors' following for this first M3 and, even though more than seventeen thousand were built, prices for some of the most prized editions are approaching six-figure dollar values. Evidence enough that this is truly one of the greats.

A Rare Misstep: The E31 M850 CSi and M8

Wrong turns and missteps are rare in BMW's history, but the 1989 850i is certainly one of them. A clue comes in the big coupé's model code: E31 places it chronologically between the E30 3-Series launched in 1982 and the second-generation 7-Series, the E32, which debuted in 1986. Why the multiyear delay?

Though it was intended as a technology flagship incorporating an unprecedented level of innovation, the 850's complexity was not the only issue. Management and marketing hesitancy were major factors, too, confirmed by the later revelation that a high-powered M8 version had been developed by the Motorsport engineering team, only to be canceled at the last minute.

Instead, the model launched in spring 1990 as the 850i, powered by the big V-12 engine from the 7-Series and equipped with every technical trick in BMW's book. These included active rear axle kinematics to improve high-speed stability, frameless door windows that lowered a few millimeters when the door handle was touched, and one of the first deployments of a six-speed manual transmission on a production car. It was an impressive specification, with a refined 300 horsepower and rapid autobahn pace, but, as with the original 633i it replaced, the thrill factor was largely absent. It felt big and heavy and the packaging was poor, and the general reaction was one of regret for what might have been.

A hint of that potential came three years later in the shape of the 850CSi. Though it didn't carry any M branding, this model was actually a product of the Motorsport engineering team. The twenty-four-valve engine was enlarged to 5.6 liters and its compression raised to 9.8:1—enough to boost power to 380 horsepower and cut the 0–100 kilometer-per-hour acceleration time to under six seconds. The CSi also featured strengthened suspension, quicker steering, and quadruple exhausts. It was also one of the first cars to have a dash-mounted control to adjust throttle sensitivity. The new version gleaned slightly better press reports but did little to nudge the sluggish sales graph upward. Many commentators preferred the lighter, less front-heavy 840i V-8 that came a year later. But all must have been left with the same thought: how sensational would the car have been in M8 form, complete with its enlarged, forty-eight-valve V-12 engine pumping out more than 550 horsepower? Only the privileged few got to try the prototypes, but at least the S70 engine's legacy lived on: it was the starting point for Paul Rosche when he began development of the 636 horsepower V-12 that made the McLaren F1 the fastest road car in the world for fifteen years.

By this time, however, BMW and its Motorsport engineers had bigger fish to fry. The company was about to plunge into a decade of turmoil with the purchase of Rover, and BMW Motorsport GmbH morphed into M GmbH with a broader and more aggressive commercial remit. As we will see in chapter 6, M engineers were really hitting their stride and setting the scene for a series of all-time greats.

Many saw the 850i as a wrong turn for BMW, its heavyweight V-12 engine providing grand-touring comfort but not the responsive thrills the brand's enthusiasts sought in a big coupé. The later 850CSi, developed by Motorsport Division, addressed that with more power and a tauter chassis, but BMW declined to give it an M8 badge.

M6351CSi & M6 (E24)

Model name and code	
M635i/M6, E24	
Claim to fame	
First road car to wear M badge; uses M1's 24-valve engine; a fabulous, elegant grand tourer	
Years in production	
1983–1988	
Number built	
5,331	
Launch price	
DM 89,500 (€45,750)	
Engine code and type	
M88/3, straight six, DOHC 24-valve, Bosch fuel injection	
Displacement, cc	
3,453	
Peak power hp @ rpm	
286@6,500	
Max torque, Nm @ rpm	
340@4,500	
Transmission and drive	
5-speed manual, rear	
Suspension, front	
MacPherson struts	
Suspension, rear	
Semi-trailing arms, coil springs	
Body styles	
Two-door coupé	
Curb weight, kg	
1,510	
Max speed (km/h) and 1–100 km/h (sec)	
255; 6.4	

Production by year

1988	406
1987	1,442
1986	602
1985	1,477
1984	1,399
1983	5
Grand total	5,331

M535i & M5 (E28)

Model name and code	
M535i, E28	M5, E28

Claim to fame	
Body-kitted 535i was not a Motorsport product but paved the way for the authentic M5	First genuine hand-built M Car had a sober exterior but staggering performance thanks to M1's 24-valve engine; high price reflected huge engineering effort

Years in production	
1984–1988	1984–1988

Number built	
10,119	7,468

Launch price	
DM 49,400 (€25,250)	DM 80,750 (€41,300)

Engine code and type	
M30B34, straight six, SOHC 12-valve, Bosch fuel injection	M88/S38, straight six, DOHC 24-valve, Bosch fuel injection

Displacement, cc	
3,430	3,453

Peak power hp @ rpm	
218@5,200	286@6,500

Max torque, Nm @ rpm	
310@4,000	340@4,500

Transmission and drive	
5-speed manual, rear, limited slip differential	5-speed manual, rear, 25% limited slip differential

Alternate transmission	
Close-ratio 5-speed manual; 4-speed ZF automatic	n/a

Suspension, front	
MacPherson struts	MacPherson struts, gas-filled dampers

Suspension, rear	
Semi-trailing arms, coils	Semi-trailing arms, coils, gas dampers

Body styles	
Four-door sedan	Four-door sedan

Curb weight, kg	
1,414	1,430

Max speed (km/h) and 1–100 km/h (sec)	
230; 7.2	245; 6.5

Production by year (M5)

1988	36
1987	1,818
1986	2,188
1985	3,380
1984	46
Grand total	7,468

For a key to specification tables, see page 221

M3 (E30)

Model name and code		
M3, E30	M3 Evolution II, E30	M3 Sport Evolution, E30

Claim to fame

The true father of the M bloodline: raw, responsive, thrilling racer for the road;
a winner wherever it went and still highly prized for its hard-core driving experience

Years in production		
1986–1989	1989–1990	1989–1991

Number built		
17,970 (all versions)	1,512	600

Launch price		
DM 59,800 (€30,575)	–	DM 93,250 (€47,675)

Engine code and type		
S14B23, straight four, DOHC 16-valve, Bosch digital motor electronics	S14B23, straight four, DOHC 16-valve, Bosch digital motor electronics	S14B25, straight four, DOHC 16-valve, Bosch digital motor electronics

Displacement, cc		
2,302	2,302	2,467

Peak power hp @ rpm		
200@6,750	220@6,750	238@7,000

Max torque, Nm @ rpm		
240@4,750	245@4,750	240@4,600

Transmission and drive		
5-speed manual close ratio, rear, 25% limited slip differential	5-speed manual close ratio, rear, 25% limited slip differential	5-speed manual close ratio, rear, 25% limited slip differential

Alternate transmission		
5-speed overdrive (US)	5-speed overdrive (US)	5-speed overdrive (US)

Suspension, front		
MacPherson struts	MacPherson struts	MacPherson struts

Suspension, rear		
Semi-trailing arms, coils	Semi-trailing arms, coils	Semi-trailing arms, coils

Body styles		
Two-door sedan and convertible	Two-door sedan	Two-door sedan

Curb weight, kg		
1,200 (Convertible: 1,360)	1,200	1,200

Max speed (km/h) and 1–100 km/h (sec)		
235; 6.7	241; 6.7	248; 6.5

Production by year (all models)

1991	300
1990	2,600
1989	2,721
1988	3,556
1987	6,396
1986	2,396
1985	1
Grand total	17,970

850 CSi (E31)

Model name and code

850 CSi, E31

Claim to fame

V-12 flagship was big on innovation but failed to convince as a sports car

Years in production

1992–1996

Number built

1,510

Launch price

DM 180,000 (€92,000)

Engine code and type

S70B56, V-12 SOHC 24-valve, Bosch Motronic engine management

Displacement, cc

5,576

Peak power hp @ rpm

380@6,300

Max torque, Nm @ rpm

550@4,000

Transmission and drive

6-speed manual, rear, limited slip differential

Suspension, front

MacPherson strut

Suspension, rear

Multilink incorporating active axle kinematics

Body styles

Two-door coupé

Curb weight, kg

1,880

Max speed (km/h) and 1–100 km/h (sec)

250 (restricted); 6.0

Production by year

1993	385
1992	1,125
Grand total	1,510

THE 1990s

HITTING THE BIG TIME

6

Six-cylinder M3 and V-8 M5 raise the dynamic benchmark ever higher

On the road, the second-generation M3 came across as a more grown-up performer, swapping the hyperactive responses of its predecessor for the long-legged pace of a luxurious Gran Turismo.

The second-generation M5 in 1988 saw a significant step-up in performance, in sophistication, and in style. In 1992 a Touring station wagon version was added.

FOR BMW, THE 1990S WERE a time of profound change. When the decade dawned, the company was an industrious and well-respected German carmaker, with three profitable premium product lines plus a couple of minor niche models. With annual sales creeping past half a million units, its manufacturing base was still firmly rooted in Germany, but it was a successful exporter to most of the rest of the world.

Fast-forward to the turn of the millennium, however, and BMW had become the center of a global empire, responsible for a top-to-bottom spectrum of scores of models under six different brands. Now selling upward of 1.1 million cars a year, it was also manufacturing in the US, the UK, and Austria. There was just one fly in the ointment: the agonizing tipping point as BMW managers struggled to decide how to extricate the company from a mess of its own making—the purchase of Rover in 1994. All the while, BMW Motorsport GmbH had remained aloof from the squabbling, an oasis of calm engineering excellence untroubled by the industrial upheavals and personality clashes going on elsewhere. This enabled M to continue to do what it had always done best: produce superbly engineered high-performance versions of already excellent BMW products—albeit with a couple of quirky, controversial turns thrown in for good measure.

E34 M5: Sober Business Suit Packs a Knockout Punch

One of the frustrations of being a regular and committed buyer of M Cars is the length of time it takes for the Motorsport version to appear after the base car has made its public debut. With the E30 M3, it had been four very long years, perhaps because a racing program was also involved, and the wait had been only slightly shorter for the very first M5, based on the E28.

Given the dramatic success of that car, not to mention the waiting lists that quickly sprang up, its successor could not come soon enough—especially as the standard new E34 5-Series, with its fresh 7-Series–like styling, had been attracting rave reviews. Sure enough, the second-generation M5 was revealed in the autumn of 1988, barely two years into the life of the E34. It marked another milestone in the evolution of the M5 ethos, which, it should be remembered, still had no equivalent, even a distant one, among competitor brands.

On the face of it, the Motorsport engineers had stuck to the same winning formula of maximum discretion, applying only minimal aerodynamic touches to the four-door body. One technical talking point was the unique "turbo" wheel design in which a special inner magnesium rotor channeled additional airflow inward to cool the brakes.

Under the hood, the S38 B36 engine was further evolved, an increase in stroke (through a forged-steel crankshaft) taking capacity to 3,535cc. Also new was M's first variable-length inlet manifold, designed to enable strong low-rev response without compromising top-end power. Some 315 horsepower was generated at a heady 6,900 rpm, guaranteeing a vivid adrenaline rush in the sub-6.3-second dash to 100 kilometers per hour, and onward to the regulated top speed of 250 kilometers per hour. Three years into the M5's run, the engine was enlarged again to 3.9 liters, making it BMW's biggest-ever six, and power rose to 340 horsepower at the same rpm. A surprise came in 1992 when BMW presented a Touring station wagon version, and in 1994 a six-speed manual became the standard transmission.

▲ Enlarged to 3.6 and later 3.8 liters, the S38 straight six benefited from a variable-length inlet manifold for strong low-down torque with no sacrifice in its searing top-end power, which peaked at 340 horsepower for a 5.9 sec dash to 100 km/h.

▼ This E34 generation of M5s was assembled largely by hand at BMW Motorsport's home facility at Garching, near the main Munich complex.

Keeping a low profile: even as a spectacularly high performer, the M5 has never felt the need to boast about its power with visual add-ons. Inside, likewise, the effect is discreetly luxurious rather than race inspired.

To the chagrin of North American customers, however, the M5 was discontinued for the region in 1993, purportedly because the just-released 540i, with its 4-liter V-8 engine, produced a similar level of power to the Motorsport straight six. To make amends, the company came up with a limited run of two hundred 540i Sport models that combined the M-spec chassis upgrades with the V-8 engine; some even had the six-speed transmission.

All E34 M5 models featured M GmbH's familiar but thoroughgoing suite of chassis upgrades, with stiffer springs, dampers, and anti-roll bars, along with the latest elastokinematics on the rear axle to aid high-speed stability. Right from the start, the results were sensational—and it was evident that this 1989 offering was an even more remarkable combination of smooth and easy everyday driving and intoxicating power and performance when roused. But perhaps the most telling verdicts come in the words of contemporary commentators, such as *Motor Sport*'s William Kimberley:

> Its performance seems to belie its staid exterior. A stunning 0–60 mph time of 6.3 seconds puts the car into the supercar league, but the performance does not stop there, for it just goes on and on. The top speed is electronically controlled so as not to exceed 155 mph, but on its way to there, it will pass almost every other make of car with the exception of just a few exotic, and very expensive, supercars.

> Not only is it one of the best cars to have left the Munich factory, but to have left any factory anywhere at any time, whether as the fastest production four-door saloon, as BMW claims, or as anything else. The only problem now facing the BMW engineers is just how the hell do they follow it up, for they have now set themselves a standard which will be a hard act to follow.

Needless to say, as we will see at the end of this chapter, BMW did indeed manage to trump this high-point M5 with its 1998 E39 generation—but it took a thundering V-8 engine to do it.

E36: The M3 Grows Up, No Longer the Noisy Rebel

BMW's third-generation 3-Series, the E36, had struck a different and more controversial note when it was unveiled in 1990, something that seemed to symbolize the spirit of the changing times. The futuristic FIZ research center had just opened and, to go with it, here was a new look, complete with faired-in headlamps—never mind the squeals of protest from flustered purists. The broader industry was in flux, too, with Porsche nearly bankrupt and Mercedes-Benz posting huge losses. But BMW, though still financially healthy, had its own internal changes to process: the departure of CEO Eberhard von Kuenheim, the figure who had scooped the company up and steered it to astonishing success over a twenty-three-year growth streak; and the arrival in the design studios of a certain American by the name of Chris Bangle. More of him later.

All of this served as the background for a further surprise—and for once it was delivered by BMW Motorsport GmbH itself. With the outgoing E30 M3 still winning races and its stock riding high among the enthusiast community, many had expected its successor to build on that highly successful formula of a razor-sharp, race-derived engine and an engagingly hard-edged chassis honed over many years of competition experience. But instead of a raw and ready racer barely toned down for the public road, the new E36 M3 presented itself as the polar opposite: it was a sophisticated GT coupé, rather than a sedan, and it came complete with a big, smooth six-cylinder engine. So in that sense it seemed to be more in the tradition of the big six-cylinder CSi coupés than a faithful follow-up to its lightweight four-cylinder predecessor.

The exhausts say it all: For its 1998 incarnation the M5 switched to V-8 power, making it the founding member of the 400 horsepower sports sedan club. Many consider this third generation to be the finest of all M5s.

As with the first-generation M3, the addition of a convertible variant broadened the model's appeal toward the luxury and leisure sector. A sedan was added, too, but the coupé was always the strongest seller.

Any misgivings soon evaporated once the key was turned, the big engine warmed up, and the throttle floored right up to the 7,250 rpm red line. This car was very fast, but in a very different way. What helped considerably was the fact that it was based on a much better car than its predecessor: notably, the new E36 range already benefited from better weight balance and the innovative Z-axle rear suspension for more benign ride and handling. Motorsport engineers had worked their magic on the standard M50 motor to turn it into the M3's S50 B30, giving an impressive 286 horsepower at 7,000 rpm, thanks in part to VANOS variable valve timing on the inlet side. Meanwhile, the chassis department specified wider tracks, stiffer springs, dampers and anti-roll bars, and variable-ratio power steering.

In an emphatic contrast to the outgoing car, there were no signs of race-style flared arches, spoilers, or splitters. The only visible differences vis-à-vis the standard car were the lower ride height, dedicated wheel designs carrying wider tires, discreetly sculpted sills, and a rear diffuser. The M3 had taken lessons from the bigger M5 and was clearly no longer the noisy rebel: it had grown up and grown respectable, and its fresh focus was reflected in the fact that the coupé was quickly joined by sedan and convertible models to broaden its appeal.

It was a strategy that paid off handsomely: even though initial reactions, especially from the specialist press, were less than enthusiastic, the new M3 sold over seventy thousand units in its six-year lifetime, more than four times the total of its single-shape

The limited-edition M3 GT of 1994 was a homologation special with an engine uprated to 295 horsepower, lowered and stiffened suspension, and some extra aero parts. All four hundred examples were finished in British racing green.

One of a kind: BMW Motorsport engineers developed an M3-engined version of the Compact hatchback for the 50th birthday of *auto, motor und sport* magazine in 1996. But despite reportedly startling performance figures, it was never put into production.

forebear. It mattered little to the typical buyer that the new car was some 20 percent heavier, that its steering was judged less communicative, or that the chassis responses were less trigger happy: the spectacular jewel of the six-cylinder engine dominated everything, delivering a jetlike surge of acceleration that culminated in an intoxicating scream as the red line approached. It became more of a straightline car than one for smaller, twistier roads.

Yet the step-up in sophistication was immense, and this was reinforced for the 1996 model year when a further engine iteration—the S50 B32—brought an enlargement to 3.2 liters, with lightweight pistons, VANOS variable valve timing to all twenty-four valves (themselves now bigger), and even more advanced engine electronics. The

outcome was a prodigious 321 horsepower at a decidedly racy 7,400 rpm—the first time a roadgoing BMW engine had given more than 100 horsepower per liter. It was claimed that this engine incorporated experience gained on the McLaren F1 V-12 project, a 6-liter unit that also broke the 100 horsepower-per-liter barrier. Allied to the new engine was a six-speed gearbox, and half a second was shaved off the earlier car's 0–100 kilometer-per-hour acceleration time of 6.0 seconds.

While BMW's M3 offer for Europe was clear and well received, its policy for the US led to uncharacteristic confusion and a rare spat. Initially, BMW North America declined to take the M3 on grounds of cost and emissions compliance. However, a concerted letter-writing campaign by the BMW Owners Club forced a rethink—though the car they finally got for the 1995 model year was much less powerful at just 240 horsepower. To save money, the S50's characteristic individual throttle bodies had been sacrificed, as had the continuous element of the variable valve timing. Worse, the rev limit was cut to 6,000 rpm to allow the inclusion of the automatic transmission supposedly demanded by Stateside customers. The chassis settings were preserved, though.

The six-speed transmission soon gave rise to another development whose acronym, SMG, would remain a notorious bone of contention within the M community for many years. The Sequential Manual Gearbox first appeared in early 1997, its mission to combine the fast shifting and sportiness of a manual box with the ease of driving of an automatic. This was important for the US market and also reflected the M3's growing role as a status vehicle as well as a sporting tool. But the grafting on of electrohydraulic control to the once manual six-speed to eliminate the clutch pedal and simplify routine driving did not go down well: early cars were jerky and hesitant to drive. Even when prompted to shift manually by a push on the shift lever, they could be slow in their reactions. The SMG went through two further iterations (in the E46 M3 and, finally, the E60 M5), stirring up arguments in each instance. It was finally abandoned in 2008 in favor of dual-clutch transmissions.

Three principal E36 M3 special editions were produced. The M3 GT, with 400 made in 1993, was a homologation model with the engine retuned to give 295 horsepower. The chassis settings were stiffened, the doors moved to aluminum to save weight, and all were finished in British racing green. The M3 Lightweight was a race model for US buyers that was stripped of its comfort equipment and insulation to help make the most of its 240 horsepower, while the Individual was a runout model with unique aero parts. Just two hundred were built, and other markets such as Canada and Australia had their own limited editions too.

Reflecting its broader lineup of body styles, the regular E36 family was available in no fewer than seven different shapes if, in addition to the Touring station wagon, the closely related Compact hatchback and Z3 roadster and Z3 coupé sports cars are included. Of these, only the Touring escaped the attention of the Motorsport engineers: the Z3M is covered below, but the stubby M Compact was an interesting one-off that never made it into production. It was created specially for the fiftieth birthday of Germany's *auto, motor und sport* magazine and posted some startling performance figures, reaching 100 kilometers per hour in a reported 5.2 seconds.

▲ ▶ Slotting the potent six-cylinder M3 engine into the previously docile Z3 Roadster resulted in a sports car of spectacular performance but tricky dynamics; the later Z3M Coupé was equally rapid but better behaved.

An Excess of Power: The E36/7 and 36/8 Z3M Roadster and Coupé

Launched in the autumn of 1995, the Z3 marked a number of important departures for BMW. It was the company's first two-seater roadster since the quirky and short-lived Z1 of 1988 and the landmark 507 thirty years before that. Indeed, the Z3's voluptuous styling paid profuse tribute to the latter, right down to the curvaceous waistline and the BMW-badged air vents in the flanks. More importantly, it was built in the company's then-new factory in Spartanburg, South Carolina, making it the first ever BMW to be manufactured entirely outside of Germany.

Technically, it was built on the engineering platform of the current E36 3-Series, but with one important difference: instead of using that car's acclaimed (but pricey) Z-axle rear suspension, it employed a simpler system that reflected the previous generation's design. It was a decision BMW may have had cause to regret, as early press reports were critical of the Z3's dynamics and rigidity. Unhelpfully, the launch models were all low-powered 1.8- and 1.9-liter fours, even though there was clearly plenty of space under the long, louvered hood for a full-size straight six.

Those sixes did arrive by the next year, and from then it was an open question whether an M version would be added too. Evidently some dissent was brewing within BMW's engineering fraternity as to the wisdom of putting such a potent engine in a chassis that might not be sophisticated enough to cope with that power—but marketing eventually won out and the M Roadster was presented at the Geneva show in spring 1996.

It looked broader and chunkier than the standard Z3, and a dramatic feature was the quadruple exhaust array at the rear, which forced the repositioning of the license plate to the rear panel. For European customers, the much-loved S50 B32 engine from the M3 was under the hood, offering its individual throttle bodies and double VANOS continuously variable valve timing—and of course the small matter of 321 horsepower at 7,400 rpm, in a car that barely breached the 1,300-kilogram mark. US buyers, by contrast, were only offered the much simpler S52, without the double VANOS and giving just 240 horsepower.

Understandably, the chassis components were all substantially uprated, and the rear suspension and subframe gained extra reinforcements. Inside the two-seater cockpit there were more instruments, more chrome, and, in later models, more leather. Absent from initial Roadster models was any form of electronic traction or stability control, which made them perhaps rather more exciting to drive than BMW had intended. Certainly, this was a light but very powerful car that demanded great respect with the throttle pedal, especially in wet weather. In this sense, it brought back memories of the 2002 Turbo and also lent credence to the reported misgivings of those senior engineers. Before long, ASC+T traction control was added, but there were also bigger developments afoot, led by those same engineers who were determined to do justice to the M badge in the Z.

The result, unveiled at the 1998 Frankfurt show, caused shock and awe in equal measure. On the revolving platform sat an oddly proportioned amalgam, with a

truncated hatchback cabin grafted onto the Roadster's long snout and windshield. The rear screen was nearly vertical, adding to the impression that the car was as wide as it was long, and again the quad exhausts added to the custom tuner impression. Interestingly, Marcus Syring, the Coupé's chief designer, revealed in an interview for this book that one of his principal inspirations for the new version was that British sports car icon of the 1960s, the MGB, and in particular the GT coupé version in which Italian design house Pininfarina had a hand. "I wanted to provide a modern interpretation," he said, "with a bit of usability, bigger trunk space, and so on." The engineering impetus behind the M Coupé, as it was labeled, was to provide a more rigid structure than the open Roadster could offer. It worked, at least for those who could stomach the quirky looks: this car was as dramatically quick as the open model, but its dynamics were far tauter and more precise. As with the Roadster, the M Coupé had the specific, lower-powered S52 engine for the US and the more potent S50 for other markets. Both models were briefly discontinued, however, only to return some months later with a brand-new engine for all markets: the S54, evolved from the European E46 M3's unit, and fitted with all the most sophisticated cam and control technology to give an impressive 325 horsepower.

This late improvement allowed both models to go out on a relative high in 2002 and clear the stage for the Z4 not long after. If the Z3 proved anything, it was that weak underpinnings are rarely the best starting point for a truly credible M Car—and that this, the quirky M Coupé aside, was not the M Division's finest hour.

E39: V-8 Power Makes for an All-Time Great M5

Many contend that this, the E39 generation, is one of the very finest M5s of all. Others go further and insist that this car deserves a place as one of the all-time greats in M-Car mythology. Either way, the E39 is without question a special incarnation of the M5, and it is memorable as the model that first introduced eight-cylinder engines to the line.

Since the E39 M5 in 1998, quadruple exhaust tailpipes have become a signature feature of all M-Cars. As always with the M5, however, the overall presentation was discreet and unaggressive, despite the 400 horsepower on tap.

With the previous generation M5 having been phased out in 1995 when the new E39-shape 5-Series line was introduced, there was a frustrating gap of almost four years while M GmbH was developing the new M5, during which time the nameplate was absent from the BMW lineup. But it was worth the wait: the extra engineering time allowed the step-up to the bigger, bulkier engine to be achieved seamlessly— and it was palpably a case of right first time. So right, in fact, that almost no running changes were made to this M5 over the course of its four-and-a-half years in production at the main Dingolfing plant. This contrasted with the previous M5s, which were largely hand-built by Motorsports GmbH at its Garching base.

There were significant obstacles to overcome, not least of which was the committed straight six fan base among M enthusiasts: many were so taken with the fabulous smoothness, the potency, and the thrilling sound of the high-revving sixes in the M3 and outgoing M5 that the move to V-8 power seemed like treason. On the plus side, the all-aluminum V-8's shorter length allowed it to be placed further back in the chassis for more centralized weight distribution, and there was the promise of even greater power and torque.

The standard E39 5-Series was already highly regarded for its quality, dynamics, comfort, and, in most versions, performance. The suspension, much of which already used aluminum components, was strengthened and stiffened; at the rear some conventional bushings were replaced by steel ball joints in the interest of maximum precision; springs were uprated and shortened for a lower ride height; and the specific M wheels and tires were wider at the rear in order to optimize balance under power.

Visual cues were, as usual, discreet: a subtly bigger grille surround, minimal sill extensions, and wider wheels. Discreet, at least until you saw the car from the back. With a quartet of exhausts rising from the diffuser and the wide-set tires clearly visible outboard of the car's flanks, the rear view showed how seriously this M5 meant business.

In typical M5 fashion, the external style was calm and subtle, and the interior a model of restraint. Note the rev counter, where the red line advances as the engine warms from cold.

Once more, the engine proved the star of the show. Based on the 4.4-liter M62 from the 540i, the Motorsport-fettled S62 was enlarged to 4,941cc, equipped with full double VANOS on each bank, along with special pistons giving an 11.0:1 compression ratio. The individual throttle bodies for each cylinder were controlled in two stages by the M Driving Dynamics system operated by the driver, and twin scavenge pumps in the semi-dry sump oil system took care of lubrication needs under sustained high-g cornering. The S62's headline horsepower figure was a talking point too: at precisely 400 it signaled the M5 as the first four-door sedan to reach this landmark number. Channeling this huge output to the rear limited slip differential were a six-speed manual transmission (no automatic offered) and a reinforced clutch. To keep everything in check, this was the first M Car with Dynamic Stability Control (DSC). Importantly for track-day drivers, the system could be switched off.

On the road, any concerns that the move to eight-cylinder power would turn the M5 into a lumpy, US-style muscle-car V-8 with no appetite for revs were swiftly dismissed. For sure, there was plenty of low-down grunt and a pleasing rumble from the quad exhausts to accompany it, but this one had a seemingly endless stream of power as the revs soared and the crescendo built. This was a seriously and addictively powerful car, one that gained speed so rapidly—0–100 kilometers per hour in as little 4.8 seconds in the hands of some magazine testers—that it demanded a close eye on the speedometer to avoid arriving at the next bend far too fast. Fortunately, however, the brakes and the chassis were more than up to the job and the sense of driver involvement was intense—in contrast to later cars where all-encompassing digital electronics seemed to sabotage the authenticity of the messages being relayed up from the road. True to the M5 tradition, the car was the model of refinement and decorum when being driven gently.

A single high-luxury specification equipped the comfy cabin with everything the contemporary customer could ask for. One particular delight was the M instrument pack where the rev counter's red line gradually rose as the engine warmed up from a cold start, reaching 7,000 rpm when the motor was at full operating temperature. Just like the E46 M3 (see chapter 7), with which it overlapped in production, the E39 M5 represents a high-water mark in the evolution of genuinely involving "pure" supercar-performance BMW M Cars in the predigital era of automobile engineering. And, for that, it does indeed deserve to be celebrated as one of the all-time greats in M's back catalog.

The move to a 4.4-liter V-8 with the E39 generation gave the M5 a huge spectrum of effortless performance, with its refinement diluting the sense of speed. The upgraded chassis and brakes made extensive use of lightweight aluminum, enabling the big sedan to lap the Nürburgring in 8 minutes 20 seconds. The S62 engine, first to break the 400-horsepower barrier, was a development of that powering the 540i.

M5 (E34)

Model name and code	
M5, E34 (3.6)	M5, E34 (3.8)

Claim to fame	
Follow-up to original M5 was even faster, more refined, and more discreet in its appearance	

Years in production	
1988–1992	1992–1995

Number built	
12,254 (total)	

Launch price	
DM 101,800 (€52,000)	DM 120,000 (€61,400)

Engine code and type	
S38B36, straight six, DOHC 24-valve; Bosch fuel injection	S38B38, straight six, DOHC 24-valve; Bosch fuel injection

Displacement, cc	
3,535	3,795

Peak power hp @ rpm	
315@6,900	340@6,900

Max torque, Nm @ rpm	
360@4,300	400@4,750

Transmission and Drive	
5-speed manual, rear	5-speed manual, rear

Suspension, front	
MacPherson strut	MacPherson strut

Suspension, rear	
Semi-trailing arms, coils, self-leveling dampers	Semi-trailing arms, coils, self-leveling dampers

Body styles	
Four-door sedan	Four-door sedan

Curb weight, kg	
1,670	1,650

Max speed (km/h) and 1–100 km/h (sec)	
250 (limited); 6.3	250; 5.9

Production by year (all models)	
1995	334
1994	600
1993	982
1992	2,318
1991	2,261
1990	3,089
1989	2,339
1988	331
Grand total	12,254

M3 (E36)

Model name and code	
M3, E36 (3.0)	M3, E36 (3.2)

Claim to fame	
Faster and more refined second-generation M3 swaps four cylinders for six but loses raw, racy edge in process; huge sales vindicate BMW's decision	

Years in production	
1992–1995	1995–1999

Number built	
71,242 (all versions)	

Launch price	
DM 80,000 (€40,900)	DM88,500 (€45,250)

Engine code and type	
S50B30, straight six, DOHC 24-valve; variable inlet timing	S50B32, straight six, DOHC 24-valve; full variable valve timing

Displacement, cc	
2,990	3,201

Peak power hp @ rpm	
286@7,000	321@7,400

Max torque, Nm @ rpm	
329@3,600	350@3,250

Transmission and Drive	
5-speed manual, rear	6-speed manual, rear

Alternative transmission	
n/a	SMG sequential

Suspension, front	
MacPherson struts, lower wishbones	MacPherson struts, lower wishbones

Suspension, rear	
Trailing arms, control arms, coil springs	Trailing arms, control arms, coil springs

Body styles	
Four-door sedan, two-door coupé and convertible	Four-door sedan, two-door coupé and convertible

Curb weight, kg	
1,460 (coupé)	1460 (coupé)

Max speed (km/h) and 1–100 km/h (sec)	
250; 6.0	250; 5.5

Production by year (all models)	
1999	5,987
1998	11,590
1997	11,911
1996	11,788
1995	11,970
1994	10,761
1993	6,715
1992	520
Grand total	71,242

For a key to specification tables, see page 221

M Roadster & M Coupé (E36/7-36/8)

Model name and code

M Roadster, E36/7 · · · · · · · · · · · · · · · · · M Coupé, E36/8

Claim to fame

A rough diamond: overpowered and edgy to drive; shock-styled Coupé is better behaved; not M's finest hour, but Z3Ms are developing a following

Years in production

1996–2002

Number built

21,613 (all versions)

Launch price

DM 91,500 (€46,800) · · · · · · · · · · · · · · · DM 95,000 (€48,575)

Engine code and type

S50B32, straight six, DOHC 24-valve, variable valve timing, Siemens fuel injection	S50B32, straight six, DOHC 24-valve, variable valve timing, Siemens fuel injection

Displacement, cc

3,210 · 3,210

Peak power hp @ rpm

321@7,400 (later 325) · · · · · · · · · · · · · 321@7,400 (later 325)

Max torque, Nm @ rpm

350@3,250 · 350@3,250

Transmission and Drive

5-speed manual, rear · · · · · · · · · · · · · · 5-speed manual, rear

Suspension, front

MacPherson struts, lower wishbones · · · MacPherson struts, lower wishbones

Suspension, rear

Semi-trailing arms, minibloc coil springs · · Semi-trailing arms, minibloc coil springs

Curb weight, kg

1,350 · 1,375

Max speed (km/h) and 1–100 km/h (sec)

250; 5.4 · 250; 5.4

Production by year (all models)

2002	698
2001	2,263
2000	2,595
1999	6,022
1998	7,943
1997	2,032
1996	60
Grand total	21,613

M5 (E39)

Model name and code

M5, E39

Claim to fame

High point for M5 as V-8 power turns it into a 400 hp big bruiser; massive, easy performance, sober exterior, not too many electronics

Years in production

1997–2003

Number built

20,482

Launch price

DM 140,000 (€71,600)

Engine code and type

S62, 90-degree V-8, DOHC 32-valve, variable valve timing; Siemens fuel injection

Displacement, cc

4,941

Peak power hp @ rpm

400@6,600

Max torque, Nm @ rpm

500@3,800

Transmission and Drive

6-speed manual, rear; DSC dynamics control

Suspension, front

Double-pivot MacPherson struts, lower wishbones, coils

Suspension, rear

Multilink axle with twin trailing arms, transverse links, lower control arms, coils

Body styles

Four-door sedan

Curb weight, kg

1,720

Max speed (km/h) and 1–100 km/h (sec)

250; 5.3

Production by year

2003	1,512
2002	2,412
2001	4,630
2000	5,824
1999	5,425
1998	678
1997	1
Grand total	20,482

THE
2000s
PEAK PERFORMANCE, PEAK COMPLEXITY

7

More cylinders, more revs, more power, more speed—and arguably the best M3 of all

The E46-generation M3, which debuted in 1999, is generally regarded as the cream of the crop—especially in its rare and even pricier CSL form.

The M3 CSL was lighter and more powerful than the regular E46 M3. Agile, pure, and tactile, and with a fabulous engine, it is highly prized by enthusiasts as perhaps the best M3 of all.

IT'S PRACTICALLY WRITTEN into the constitution of BMW's M Division that each new model must deliver a clear improvement over the car that went before it. Of course, what qualifies as an improvement is a notion that has evolved gradually over the years, and now, in the rapidly electrifying 2020s, the upcoming generations of M Cars are expected to chase their gains in new areas such as agility, responsiveness, and lateral acceleration—in other words, cornering prowess.

Wind back to just before the millennium, however, and the focus for the M engineers was rather different, and also a lot easier to understand. The V-8–powered M5, launched in 1998, was brilliantly successful in its chosen role of huge performance clothed in a Savile Row suit. It had prompted a hasty rival from Mercedes-AMG but deflected the challenge without difficulty. To raise its game still further, though, would be a tough call.

But even though the original M3 had established the market for midsize sports sedans, BMW's advantage over challengers such as Audi's Porsche-inspired RS2 wagon and Mercedes' AMG-tuned C-Class models was no longer quite so clear-cut. As the always-awkward "second-album" follow-up to the electrifying original M3, the second-generation model had—in the eyes of many, at least—failed to match the raw thrills of its groundbreaking E30 mentor: for all its six-cylinder sophistication and prodigious straightline performance, something had been lost in its transformation into a more mainstream, more accessible hotshot sedan.

For this reason, BMW M-Division engineers, acutely conscious of their commitment always to go one better, pushed their M-magic mission further and faster for the new millennium. In so doing, they created a new generation of cars remarkable for a variety of reasons. And prominent in this tally is the model that is a prime candidate for the title of the finest M Car of all time.

E46: Sweet-Spot M3 is an All-Time Favorite

For many BMW M enthusiasts, especially those whose experience goes back more than twenty years, this is the one. The cream of the entire crop and preferable, even, to the latest M4s with twice as many horses and four times the computing power.

It's often true that the closest friends are the harshest critics—and this was doubly evident when devotees of the original M3 upgraded to its six-cylinder E36 successor in 1992. While most welcomed the greater comfort, the dramatic turbine-smooth acceleration, and the easy everyday drivability of the new model, a significant and very vocal contingent bemoaned what they felt had been lost: the pure-blooded race car feel, the hyperactive steering, the urgency of every response. The successor car, they suggested, had sold that racetrack soul in pursuit of the fatter profits that come with higher-volume sales to wealthy business types and socialites seeking snob value.

Harsh and perhaps hasty words were spoken, but BMW certainly took them to heart when it came to developing the next-generation M3, based on the E46 Coupé launched as a regular model in spring 1999. An M3 "study" was shown by the autumn of that year and, when the production M3 was revealed the following spring, it proved faithful in almost every detail to the concept. The coupé body style, with its lower and wider silhouette (no panels were shared with the sedan) already gave a more stable and securely planted stance on the road than the sedan. The M3 took this one step further with a broader grille, an aluminum hood with a pronounced power bulge, and wider front fenders to house the broader wheels and tires. Perfect finishing touches were the quadruple exhausts and neat air vent grilles set into the front wing panels, discreetly echoing those on the iconic E9 3-liter coupés of the 1970s.

The 3.2-liter straight six reached new heights of brilliance in the E46; this is the most potent Coupé-only CSL version, which upped power to 360 horsepower thanks to enhancements such as the large carbon airbox. External differences were subtle, taking a trained eye to spot. Convertible versions of the M3 were heavier but closely matched the driving thrills of Coupés.

No expense was spared in reengineering the already good E46 chassis to provide altogether higher levels of grip, handling, and responsiveness. Forged aluminum wishbones replaced the standard components to give greater front-end stiffness and a significantly wider track, while at the rear M prescribed a stronger subframe and suspension anchor points, steel ball joints, stiffer springs, dampers and anti-roll bars, and heftier half-shafts taking the drive to the wheels. The M Differential Lock was a novel Viscodrive unit codeveloped with GKN. If there was a surprise in the chassis specifications, it was that the revised steering was actually lower geared than the standard car's.

As always with a new M Car, though, the engine was the heart of the matter. Designated S54, the 3.2-liter unit was the final evolution of the familiar iron-block straight six. With revised camshafts, an 11.5:1 compression ratio, and the latest generation of electronic engine management, it boasted maximum power of 343 horsepower at 7,900 rpm. The first-time employment of an e-throttle allowed the choice of different pedal response modes, and a special semi-dry sump scavenge pump ensured there would be no oil starvation even under sustained high-g cornering.

The posted 0–100 kilometer-per-hour acceleration time was 5.2 seconds and the top speed a regulated 250 kilometers per hour. But when the price of DM 100,000 was

The M3 GTR was a homologation special for North American race series, with a 500 horsepower V-8 replacing the 3.2-liter inline six. Plans to offer a roadgoing version did not materialize.

announced, there was a collective gasp: BMW had, dramatically and quite possibly deliberately, raised the stakes by pricing the M3 firmly in Porsche territory, and not just matching the price of a basic Boxster but surpassing that of the faster and better equipped Boxster S, pegged at DM 95,000.

Those buyers who had the wherewithal to stump up Porsche cash were not disappointed. BMW had achieved the seemingly impossible: not just building still further on the thrilling power and sophistication of the outgoing car, but also silencing critics by managing to incorporate much of the raw excitement of the pioneering E30 from two generations before. Plaudits came thick and fast, extolling everything from the M3's civilized, easygoing nature in day-to-day commuting to its quality of construction, its breathtaking performance when opened up, and the fearsome scream of the engine as it clearly hungered for the tachometer's 8,000 rpm red line. If there was any hesitancy, it centered around the steering that, though great at higher speeds, felt unpromisingly light and nonsporting around town.

For BMW it was another clear case of right first time, and this is borne out by the fact that few running changes were made to the standard M3's engineering during the seven years it remained in production at the company's main Munich plant. A convertible with a power-operated soft-top joined the lineup in 2001: the substantial stiffening that M engineers judged necessary put an extra 180 kilograms onto the curb weight, adding a half second to its 0–100 kilometer-per-hour acceleration time. The SMG automated manual transmission reappeared at the same time, now in second-generation form and offering no fewer than eleven programs. One of these was a brutal Launch Control mode that optimized upshift points to give the fastest possible acceleration.

Sweet spot: this M3 generation brought back the speed, agility, and responsiveness that drivers had been craving.

A brace between the front suspension towers was added to both versions in 2002, and late in 2004 the suspension was subtly revised to reduce understeer. At the same time a Competition Pack was offered, delivering some of the chassis upgrades of the 2003 CSL (see below), such as quicker steering and an M Track mode for the DSC, which raised the threshold at which the system intervened.

A minor diversion in the E46 M3 story was the GTR version, built primarily for racing in the US American Le Mans series. Regulations required a roadgoing version to be offered, too, resulting in a wild body-kitted shape with aggressive carbon spoilers, splitters, and wheelarch extensions. Under the hood was the 4-liter V-8 from the 5-Series, tuned to give 380 horsepower. Only a handful of road versions were sold, but the race cars swept the board in the AMLS championships in 2001 and continued winning other races throughout the decade.

All in all—and with the benefit of two decades' hindsight—the E46-generation M3 represents BMW M design and engineering at its finest. It was the final flourish of the magnificent, rev-hungry straight six engine with its smooth and uninterrupted flow of torque and searing peak power. The chassis, for all its sophistication, did not rely on significant electronic intervention to give its best, leading to an inspirationally pure and genuine driving experience. Fittingly, it is easily the best-selling M model to date, with over eighty-five thousand finding buyers and almost twenty-four thousand sold in 2002, its peak year. From the vantage point of today's increasingly digital world, this M3 stands out as perhaps the last great analog, nonturbo sports car.

E46 M3 CSL: Vastly More Than the Sum of Its Parts

For a car with a limited build run of fewer than 1,400 units, one that was never sold in North America and was only available in a single specification and just two different colors, the M3 CSL enjoys a disproportionately huge influence in the BMW M universe. Indeed, it is often celebrated not just as the best M Car of its era, but of all time—no small honor, considering what had gone before and what came after.

Yet for a car that went on to be so idolized, the initial reactions at the CSL's announcement were surprisingly equivocal. The standard M3 was already so excellent that it would be hard to improve on, people reasoned. The increase in

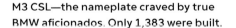

M3 CSL—the nameplate craved by true BMW aficionados. Only 1,383 were built.

power of just 17 horsepower was no big deal, and the inclusion of lightweight parts to save 110 kilograms seemed like scant justification for the appropriation of the hallowed CSL designation made famous by the big 3-liter E9 coupés. Worse, a truly shocking price tag of €85,000 in 2003 money—one-third more than the already pricey standard car—fueled the belief of some cynics that the CSL's primary mission was to perform on the balance sheet rather than on the open road.

How wrong those doubters proved to be. As so often with high-performance BMWs, the CSL was vastly more than the sum of its parts, though its case wasn't helped by the fact that it took a highly trained eye to distinguish it from the standard car. Only the lowered suspension, the larger 19-inch wheels, and the single offset circular air intake set into the lower left of the front apron marked it out at first glance.

That air inlet was an important clue to the other hidden CSL changes, for it channeled oxygen direct to an extensively revised induction system. A large carbon-look plenum occupied most of the available underhood space and was tasked with further improving engine response. The system had an internal flap that opened at higher revs and engine load, at which point, as early reviewers excitedly reported, the throaty induction note became a full-blown, sonorous howl. It has been said that the flap was necessary to pass the drive-by noise tests, something borne out by the fact that it remained fully open in Sport mode. With a rev limit raised to 8,200, the S54 B32HP gave 360 horsepower, still at 7,900 rpm, and torque increased fractionally to 370 Newton meters.

Among the chassis changes were a further lowering and stiffening of the suspension, with new componentry at the rear to increase camber. The brakes were upgraded, too, and—after a long wait—the steering ratio was quickened. What looked like discreet bodywork upgrades actually went far deeper: the roof panel was carbon fiber, saving 6 kilograms, and the trunk lid, front apron, rear diffuser, and all their supports were in lightweight composites as well. Inside, almost every comfort extra was deleted, from air conditioning on down, and the door cards were simplified to plastic moldings. But the biggest surprise was that just one transmission was offered, and that it was the SMG II, which had always received bad press from M owners.

The lighter weight and increased power helped drop the CSL's 0–100 kilometer-per-hour time to under 5 seconds. Customers with a racing license could order theirs with the speed limiter removed, giving a maximum speed of over 280 kilometers per hour. On the standard semi-racing Michelin Pilot Sport tires, the CSL set a new Nürburgring Nordschleife lap record for production four-seater cars of 7 minutes 50 seconds, compared with 8 minutes 22 seconds for the standard M3.

THE CSL FROM THE DRIVER'S SEAT

Jesse Crosse, one of the world's leading motoring journalists and a committed M3 enthusiast, was present at the international press presentation of the M3 CSL in 2003. Now, after having evaluated hundreds of performance models launched over the past three decades, he has given pride of place in his garage to a late-2003 CSL. Here is his report.

My first experience of the M3 CSL was as a journalist attending a tech day on diesel engines at BMW's Aschheim test track. The new model had been eagerly awaited, but its appearance, along with Le Mans driver Hans Stuck to give demonstration rides on the closed circuit, was a complete surprise. The CSL's nimbleness and impeccable balance were obvious even from the passenger seat and I couldn't wait to drive one.

Over the next couple of decades I did so several times—and in fact I grabbed every chance I had to get behind the wheel of one. In those days, BMW M Cars were still developed and built by a small crack team away from the main production lines, and it shows in this car.

From the driver's seat, the CSL feels completely different to the standard M3, which I owned immediately before finally managing to buy the CSL. The seating position in the wrap-around bucket seat is low and, combined with the lower ride height, gives the sensation of sitting in a race car rather than a road car. The CSL feels much lighter, more nimble and more tactile through the hands and the seat of the pants. Picking up the pace along twisty roads it comes alive and, while not twitchy, it feels sinuous and eager to change direction. On that score, the steering is far more connected to the throttle pedal with the rear end more responsive than the standard car.

The engine note is sublime, enough to eulogize over for hours and certainly something to savor. There's very little that comes close. While the automated, single-clutch manual gearbox that is the SMG doesn't compare well to a modern DCT, with understanding it's far more satisfying than it's often given credit for. In Sport mode, shifts are brutal, with a resounding clunk from the driveline when shifting at full power. But a separate button gives control of the SMG response rate on a digital readout like the reception quality on a smartphone.

When not in Sport and with the response set to fast, the SMG timing is quite predictable, and at high speeds downshifts before corners are nice and smooth. With the best will in the world, the manual gearbox (on the basic M3) isn't the greatest: it's slow and clunky to use, and has a relatively long throw.

As for the rest? The lack of sound deadening is palpable and the CSL is very sensitive to changing road surfaces transmitting plenty of tire noise into the cabin at times. On the other hand, the interior is a delicious blend of carbon fiber and Alcantara, and the CSL is a simply intoxicating car to drive in just about every respect. A couple of senior ride and handling engineers I know in the motor industry still regard the CSL's handling as a benchmark and it's an opinion that's richly deserved. Is it the best M Car ever? Quite possibly.

Journalist Jesse Crosse on his CSL: "The engine note is sublime—there's nothing else that comes close." *Courtesy of Jesse Crosse*

M5 E60/61: Max Power, Maximum Complexity, Maximum Intimidation

The high-water mark set by the E39-generation M5 launched in 1998 was always going to be a tough one to surpass. In the intervening six years, the stakes had risen dramatically and the competition was beginning to catch up. In the escalating power race, Mercedes was coming close to the M5's 400 horsepower with its AMG-tuned E-Class, while Audi had already smashed right through the 400-horsepower barrier with its RS6 thanks to a little help from Cosworth and twin turbos on its 4.2-liter V-8. Besides, BMW was by now waging war on an even more glamorous front, the Formula 1 circuits, with its near-900-horsepower V-10 engine in the back of the Grand Prix Williams.

To stay ahead of the game, the M5's successor would need decisively more power. Turbo- or supercharging the existing V-8 was technically possible, but too similar to what Mercedes and Audi were doing, and BMW's brand position at the time was one of pure, high-revving, naturally aspirated performance engines rather than peaky turbos. There was the V-12 from the 7-Series, but that was clearly too big and heavy—so the sensible compromise of going to ten cylinders beckoned. What better way to simultaneously better the outgoing model and outdo the opposition than by developing a new model that exploited BMW's unique expertise in current Formula 1 technology, taken straight from the racetrack?

This was the thinking that prompted BMW to channel vast resources into what would become M Division's most ambitious road car program to date. This marked a high point in pure mechanical engineering and, at the same time, provided a bridge to the modern era where electronic programs increasingly control how a vehicle functions, how it behaves on the road, and how it responds to the driver's commands.

By early 2004, the intricate project was ready enough to be displayed as a production-standard concept at the Geneva show that March. The new fifth-generation 5-Series had been launched the year before as the second of Chris Bangle's creations, and whatever shock value the styling originally possessed had already worn off. So the M5 revealed itself as a sensitively tweaked version of the basic Bangle shape with all its complex hollows, bulges, and cut-lines, and with sporting touches that marked it out as rather more aggressive than its predecessor, but stopping short of becoming exhibitionistic.

Understated but over-engineered: the fourth-generation M5 stayed faithful to the philosophy of keeping the exterior design subtle, but the high-revving V-10 engine and SMG transmission hit new heights of technical complexity.

The formidable 5-liter V-10 engine was inspired by Formula 1 racing and revved to over 8,000 rpm. It propelled the M5 into the 500-horsepower class for ballistic performance, but the 7-speed SMG transmission lacked the sophistication of later dual clutch systems.

When the production model was revealed that same September, it was the engineering that stole the show. M Division had thrown everything they knew at this project. The ten-cylinder engine and the seven-speed transmission were entirely new, made-to-measure designs. Beyond this, the suspension was extensively reconfigured, the steering was all new, and electronic systems gave the driver a never-before-seen ability to set up the car's dynamic parameters to his or her liking. The M5's statistics were more impressive still. The intricate race-inspired 5-liter V-10, designated S85 B50, was deliberately very over-square for searing top-end power, revving to 8,250 rpm and busting the 500 horsepower barrier on the way. M's trademark individual throttle bodies for each cylinder were operated by a separate linkage and motor for each bank of the vee. The hollow camshafts operating the forty valves were driven by chains and gears, and the crankcase's bedplate construction echoed racing practice. But where M engineers truly revealed their racing expertise was when it came to keeping the massive motor's weight down: ready for the road, it measured just 250 kilograms, exactly the same as the outgoing V-8 with fewer cylinders and 20 percent less power.

While BMW was quick to claim the engine's Formula 1 inspiration, the hardware was entirely unique to the road car; most of the F1 expertise was transferred to the domain of electronics. The MS65 engine management module contained over one thousand individual components and could carry out two hundred million calculations per second, dealing with fifty different parameters for every revolution of the crankshaft.

All this added up to an ultrapowerful luxury sedan with a huge intimidation factor, not helped by BMW's claim that without the 250 kilometer-per-hour speed limiter in place the M5 would carry on to 330 kilometers per hour. This was of great significance for UK and US buyers, as it saw a four-seater sedan demolish the 200-mile-per-hour barrier, until then the preserve of supercars such as the Ferrari F40 and McLaren F1.

Conscious of the consequences of unleashing all 507 horsepower in town or in wet conditions, the M5 always started up in its default mode of just 400 horsepower, with a push of the Power button on the dash releasing the remaining 107 horses. Adding to the fear factor was the bewildering array of decisions facing the driver: eleven modes for the SMG III gearbox, three throttle response profiles, three suspension and two steering modes, and three settings for the DSC stability control system. Fortunately, the driver's preferred combination could be stored and recalled instantly by pushing the red M button on the steering wheel.

As a dynamic machine, the M5 was theoretically excellent, with astonishing power, huge performance, and a screaming noise from its complex engine. It offered a decent ride and taut handling with the correct suspension choices, to say nothing of its first-class equipment and build quality. But in everyday practice it was something of a letdown, with the SMG III automated manual transmission alternating between hesitancy and jerkiness, the engine's explosive energy making for stressful rather than relaxing travel, and too many electronic systems to master.

Despite the superficial simplicity of the controls, the M5 introduced multiple electronic systems that were intimidatingly complex to understand and set up. The transmission alone had eleven modes and the throttle response three profiles.

As with the E34 M5 two generations back, the E60 range also included a Touring station wagon version.

One surprise was the appearance in 2007 of a Touring station wagon version. This was never sold in North America, but US buyers frustrated with the SMG III gearbox exerted pressure of their own to have a manual transmission option. Few other running changes were made to the M5 during its five years in production, though the car's complexity did lead to more reliability issues and higher servicing costs than most BMW owners were accustomed to.

In summary, the E60 M5 could be seen as a fine engineering achievement, taking the nonturbo engine further and faster than ever before. But it was also too complex for its own good, diluting the sense of driver involvement that is so important to the ethos of BMWs M Division. Historically, it sits uncomfortably on the borderline between the analog and the digital driving experience, between the extravagance of extreme engine speeds and the easier efficiency of turbocharged power. As such, could it one day be regarded as the last of the true mechanical greats, or simply as the costly folly of a technical dead end? The jury is still out.

Z4M E85/86: M's Sports Car Finds Favor Again

Bruised by the critical hammering it had received following the 1995 launch of its US-built Z3 sports car with its weedy engines and substandard chassis, BMW was taking no chances with its successor roadster, the Z4. Right from the get-go in 2003 this was a class act, with powerful six-cylinder engines, a fully resolved chassis taken from the very latest E46 3-Series (rather than an outdated model) and, of course, highly expressive styling from the pen of Chris Bangle.

▲ Second time lucky: after the mixed reception for the Z3M in 1996, BMW M was taking no chances with its Z4M follow-up. Both Roadster and Coupé were thoroughly engineered, using the latest M3 driveline and suspension.

◀ As if to prove its point, BMW issued a body-in-white image of the Z4M Coupé's structure.

Straight from the M3: the Z4M's energetic straight six gave a sizzling 343 horsepower at close on 8,000 rpm. Though the body structure was much stiffer than the earlier Z3, the Z4M's high power and low weight still called for caution on wet or uneven road surfaces.

With such a high-quality baseline, the arrival of a Z model was always assured, and the Z4M duly appeared in Roadster form at the 2006 Detroit motor show; the sleek fastback M Coupé followed two months later at the Geneva show. By the standards of the outgoing Z3 sports car generation, the visual changes for the Z4M models were discreet and subtle, the main giveaways being a deeper air dam at the front, black-finished kidney grilles recessed slightly deeper into the front apron, and a more pronounced rear diffuser complete with the now M-typical quadruple exhausts. To no one's surprise—and equally to no one's regret—the Z4M's mechanical specifications closely reflected that of the highly acclaimed E46 M3, though the S54 engine was tweaked slightly, with larger bores to displace 3,246cc and the compression raised to 11.5:1. Peak power remained at 343 horsepower at 7,900 rpm, which went a long way in a compact roadster weighing less than the M3 (though more than the lightweight CSL).

Important differences from the standard Z4's chassis specification included brakes from the M3 CSL and the upgrade to fully hydraulic power steering from the original electro-hydraulic. The suspension setup was notably stiff, even more so in the Coupé, to the extent that the car could feel skittish on bumpy or damaged roads. Two different M modes were available for the Dynamic Drive Control, offering still tauter responses for those who desired them.

The Z4 M Roadster and its Coupé cousin remained in the BMW catalog until late 2008, when it was replaced by the facelifted E89 Z4 with its single retractable hardtop body style. No M version was offered, but it did feature the seven-speed dual-clutch transmission that had debuted on the new V-8-powered E90 M3 the year before. The outgoing Z4M models were thrilling cars dominated by a fabulous engine. For sure, they had a distinct wild side, but they were a lot less polarizing—and a lot less hard-core—than their decidedly lurid Z3M predecessors.

The year 2005 saw the return of a famous nameplate in the Bangle-inspired shape of the M6. Effectively coupé and cabriolet versions of the M5 sedan, the sporting duo boasted shattering performance thanks to the screaming V-10 engine but straddled an uneasy line between pure sports cars and luxury grand tourers.

F1 Engineering with a Luxury Twist:
The E63/64 M6 Coupé and Convertible

It is three years into the twenty-first century, and the design upheaval launched by Chris Bangle with the 2001 E65 7-Series is in full swing: the whipped-up panic over the big Seven is waning, and the new 5-Series and the Z4 have kicked up much less fuss. So the speculation is now focusing on the upcoming big coupé. How closely would it reflect the highly polarizing Z9 GT Concept of 1999?

The answer came in September 2003 with the unveiling of the 645Ci, its designation reviving that of BMW's most treasured icons, the elegant Bracq-styled E24 coupé that had lasted for more than a decade from 1976. Unlike its forebear, however, the new car's lumpy looks proved more of a talking point than its engineering, which was taken straight from the E60 5-Series sedan. Following within months, the Convertible was easier on the eye, but it was the Coupé that was first to receive the M treatment, in 2005, one headline feature being its carbon roof panel. The M6 Convertible debuted in autumn 2006.

Given that the 6-Series was built on 5-Series architecture, the M specifications ran to the same purpose-built V-10 engine and complex electronic systems as the sedan, including a Power Control device that gave the choice of P400 for "just" 400 horsepower, P500 for the full 507, or P500 Sport, which was only accessible through the iDrive menu and gave similar power but with a more violent throttle response curve. Likewise, just as in the M5, the third-generation SMG III automated manual transmission gave owners a huge range of auto or manual shift options: the calibration felt more aggressive than in the sedan, with some modes delivering lightning-fast upshifts that slammed in hard under determined acceleration. As with the M5, though, a manual transmission was available as an option for North American customers.

Few running changes were made during the M6's production run of barely sixty months. Three years in, BMW offered an optional Competition Pack with lowered and further stiffened suspension, firmer three-stage dampers, and wider wheels. These models are identifiable by the two subtle ribs that flow rearward from the BMW badge on the hood. As the M6 neared the end of its run in late 2009, a Competition Edition Coupé gave a slight boost to sales that had been hit by the financial crisis. This runout model combined the Competition Pack chassis upgrades with a comprehensive luxury interior specification.

Like its M5 companion, this generation of M6 is impressive in its complex engineering and immense power and performance. Again like the M5, it was hugely potent without being the also-docile all-rounder that everyone had come to expect from M Division. And even as a pure driving machine it had some significant flaws that mark it down as technically fascinating but not yet the true classic that its namesake had been twenty years before.

More cylinders, more revs, more speed: the M3's graduation to V-8 power for the 2007 model year gave it a very different and more muscular character at low speeds but strident energy toward its 8,300 rpm red line.

From Six to Eight: E90-93 M3 Raises the Power Stakes

The power struggle between Germany's three premium automakers was playing out with particular intensity as the millennium year receded further in the rearview mirror, and both Mercedes-AMG and Audi had upped the stakes significantly in their efforts to wrest the advantage from BMW's highly regarded M3. The Mercedes C 55 AMG had trumped even the M3 CSL's power output by the simple expedient of dropping in a large V-8, and the successor model would boast an even bigger eight-cylinder. Audi, for its part, had just fielded a sweet, high-revving 4-liter V-8 of 414 horsepower for its RS4: "Look out, M3!" warned one leading magazine.

BMW had not been standing still, though. M GmbH engineers knew full well that there was no more development left in the remarkable 3.2-liter S54 straight six and that it would not pass upcoming emissions standards if pushed any further. In a dilemma uncannily similar to that faced by the fourth-generation M5, the route to the necessary higher power outputs would lead either to turbocharging (not yet in the M skill set) or to adding more cylinders.

The latter option was the obvious choice: a nonturbo would align more closely with the M ethos of sophisticated, free-revving engines with smooth power delivery, and a useful kit of parts was on hand in the shape of the M5's mighty V-10. Lopping off two of the V-10's cylinders resulted in a handily sized 4-liter V-8 giving an initial 420 horsepower at a soaring 8,300 rpm. This new engine, designated S65 B40, had nothing in common with the units found in the standard 5-Series or the M3 GTS racing special of the E46 generation.

The standard E90 3-Series sedan had debuted in 2004, to less-than-unanimous praise for its Bangle-influenced styling, especially at the rear. The E91 Touring, E92 Coupé, and E93 Convertible followed in quick succession, though in typical BMW fashion there were few body panels shared between each style. The Convertible was a particular break with tradition as it featured a retractable metal hardtop rather than a folding canvas top, giving it a less attractive profile with the roof in place.

The first sight of the fourth-generation M3 was the Coupé Concept in spring 2007. The production M3 followed in the fourth quarter, while the sedan and Convertible came in 2008. No Touring was offered, and all variants were built on BMW's main assembly lines in Regensburg.

To adapt the model for the much higher power outputs, BMW M engineers developed a strengthened front subframe and stronger strut supports, revising the geometry and widening the track in addition to stiffening the springs and allowing for three-stage adjustable Electronic Damping Control (EDC) dampers all round. At the rear, the track was widened, some bushings replaced with steel ball joints, and the springs stiffened. Also included were wider 18-inch wheels and a quicker steering rack than the standard car.

All exterior panels forward of the A-pillar were unique to the M3 to allow for the broader fenders to accommodate the wider wheel/tire combinations, and to provide additional cooling airflow for the larger powerplant. The already domed aluminum hood required a further large power bulge at the rear to clear the engine componentry and, as had become the M signature, air-exit grilles were set into the fenders just aft of the wheelarches. Coupé models had a carbon roof to save weight, and at the rear a large diffuser with mesh insert topped the quadruple exhaust outlets.

The V-8 in the E90 M3 was actually lighter than the six it replaced, and it sat further back in the chassis for better weight distribution. A welcome development was the seven-speed M-DCT dual-clutch transmission to replace the unloved SMG of the previous generation.

Inevitably, though, most of the attention focused on the engine and driveline. Running a high 12:1 compression ratio, this sophisticated V-8 was safe to 8,400 rpm. BMW had a quick retort to anyone who expressed concern that the extra cylinders would make the M3 heavier and less agile: the V-8, said M engineers, was 15 kilograms lighter than the six it replaced, and it could sit further back in the chassis to minimize the car's polar moment of inertia. The launch specifications made no mention of an SMG transmission, for good reason: a few months into production, the announcement came that the auto option for the M3 would be a dual-clutch transmission, labeled M-DCT. Supplied to BMW in seven-speed form by Getrag, the DCT had earlier been pioneered by Volkswagen on the Golf R32 and promised to be both quicker and easier to drive than a manual.

That was borne out in practice, with the manual Coupé hitting 100 kilometers per hour from standstill in just 4.8 seconds and its M-DCT–equipped companion shaving 0.2 second off that time. For the Convertible, with its 200 kilograms' greater mass, the figures were 5.3 and 5.1 seconds, respectively. In terms of maximum speed, all adhered to German industry's self-imposed limit of 250 kilometers per hour—though one source reports a US magazine's claim that the M3 would top out at 327 kilometers per hour with the limiter removed.

For drivers accustomed to the cozy neatness of the outgoing M3, the new model presented a less welcoming interior environment: the displays were separated across two different housings, and many of the electronic functions were controlled by the rotary iDrive knob on the center console. Most of the functions paralleled those on the M5, though the Power button only controlled the response curve of the throttle rather than limiting the maximum output.

At low speeds, the V-8 brought an unfamiliar rumbly sensation reminiscent of some muscle cars, but at higher speeds it came into its own with strident energy as the tachometer needle shot past the 8,000 rpm mark. The M-DCT transmission was a willing companion in this, its multiple modes being easily accessible via a plus-minus rocker switch on the console. In terms of driving precision, however, the new car came across as less exciting than its predecessor, despite its substantial power advantage. The raw edge had been diluted, and many regretted the loss of the six's creamy smoothness and incisive top end.

Around launch time there were strong rumors of a lighter and more purist CSL version on the way to address the hard-core enthusiast market, but the GTS, in Coupé form only, wasn't to appear until 2010. It was indeed lightened, to the tune of 70 kilograms, and its engine featured a longer stroke to give 4.4 liters and 450 horsepower. There were significant chassis changes, too, but all was directed toward track use and fewer than the planned one hundred and fifty were eventually sold. All were finished in bright orange, even the engine covers, and the rear seats were removed to make way for a factory-fitted roll cage.

A multitude of other special editions were produced for BMW's many national markets. All were mainly cosmetic in character, apart from the M3 CRT sedan, which was a less hard-core version of the GTS and served as a runout model for the four-door.

BMW Art Car series: Jeff Koons
The New York artist and sculptor's vivid bands of bright and contrasting colors on the 2010 M3 GT2 race car's black bodywork resulted in one of the most spectacular Art Cars of the whole series. The multicolored lines radiate from the car's front to give a powerful impression of movement and speed.

With a sales total of fewer than sixty-six thousand units in five years, the E90-generation M3 was less celebrated and less of a commercial success than its purer E46 mentor, which sold more than eighty-five thousand. With the benefit of hindsight this could be seen as the penalty of BMW chasing ever-higher numbers, becoming caught up in the weight and power spiral and adding layers of engineering complexity that did little to enhance M's core values of agility and driver engagement.

Like the V-10 M5, the V-8 M3 was something of a dead end; a technical high point, for sure, but one that also marked the end of an era where high revs, peak power, and conspicuous consumption were still the norm in performance car design. For, as we will see in chapter 9, efficiency was fast becoming the watchword post-2010 and a new, downsized turbo generation was about to take over.

The switch to a rigid metal folding hardtop for the Convertible version of the V-8 M3 did not find universal favor: it added 200 kilograms to the car's mass, blunting its performance edge, and the roof-up profile lacked the harmonious silhouette of a soft-top.

M3 & M3 CSL (E46)

Model name and code	
M3, E46	M3 CSL, E46
Claim to fame	
Arguably the cream of the M3 crop: hits sweet spot in speed, agility, response, and driver involvement	More highly focused, and perhaps the best M3 ever; light, nimble, tactile, with sublime power and purity
Years in production	
1999–2006	2003–2006
Number built	
85,766 (all models)	1,383
Launch price	
DM 100,000 (€51,950)	€85,000
Engine code and type	
S54 B32, straight six, DOHC 24-valve; variable valve timing, Bosch fuel injection	S54 B32HP, straight six, DOHC 24-valve; variable valve timing, Bosch fuel injection
Displacement, cc	
3,245	3,245
Peak power hp @ rpm	
343@7,900	360@7,900
Max torque, Nm @ rpm	
365@4,900	370@4,900
Transmission and drive	
6-speed manual, rear	6-speed SMG II sequential, rear
Alternative transmission	
6-speed SMG II sequential	n/a
Suspension, front	
MacPherson struts, lower wishbones	MacPherson struts, lower wishbones
Suspension, rear	
Multilink axle with trailing arms, transverse links, lower control arms, coils	Multilink axle with trailing arms, transverse links, lower control arms, coils
Body styles	
Two-door coupé and convertible	Two-door coupé
Curb weight, kg	
1,495	1,385
Max speed (km/h) and 1–100 km/h (sec)	
250; 5.2	250 (280 without limiter); 4.9

Production by year (all models)	
2006	4,436
2005	8,436
2004	13,246
2003	19,271
2002	23,754
2001	15,294
2000	1,300
1999	29
Grand total	85,766

Z4M (E85-86)

Model name and code
Z4M Roadster, E85, and Z4M Coupé, E86
Claim to fame
Vastly better follow-up to Z3 combined sparkling M3 drivetrain with stiff, responsive chassis, and choice of cabrio or sleek fastback coupé style; facelift model with retractable hardtop had no M version
Years in production
2004–2008
Number built
9,968
Launch price
€61,650 (Roadster)
Engine code and type
S54 B32, straight six, DOHC 24-valve; variable valve timing, Bosch fuel injection
Displacement, cc
3,246
Peak power hp @ rpm
343@7,900
Max torque, Nm @ rpm
365@4,900
Transmission and drive
6-speed manual, rear, DSC, M Differential Lock
Suspension, front
MacPherson struts, lower wishbones
Suspension, rear
Multilink axle with trailing arms, transverse links, lower control arms, coils
Body styles
Two-door convertible and coupé
Curb weight, kg
1,420 (convertible), 1,410 (coupé)
Max speed (km/h) and 1–100 km/h (sec)
250; 5.0

Production by year (all models)	
2008	619
2007	2,280
2006	6,906
2005	141
2004	22
Grand total	9,968

For a key to specification tables, see page 221

M5 (E60)

Model name and code

M5, E60/61

Claim to fame

Peak engineering complexity with manic V-10; explosive and intimidating, but too complex to deliver consistent driver enjoyment

Years in production

2003–2010

Number built

20,589 (both versions)

Launch price

£63,285 (€88,600)

Engine code and type

S85 B50, 90-degree V-10, DOHC 40-valve, variable valve timing, Siemens engine management

Displacement, cc

4,999

Peak power hp @ rpm

507@7,750

Max torque, Nm @ rpm

520@6,100

Transmission and drive

7-speed SMG III sequential, rear; DSC and M Variable Differential Lock

Alternative transmission

6-speed manual (North America only)

Suspension, front

MacPherson struts, lower wishbones

Suspension, rear

Multilink system with twin transverse links, trailing arms, tie bars, coils

Body styles

Four-door sedan and Touring station wagon

Curb weight, kg

1,755

Max speed (km/h) and 1–100 km/h (sec)

250 (restricted)/330 (claimed); 4.7

Production by year

2010	10
2009	669
2008	1,542
2007	4,793
2006	5,478
2005	7,821
2004	235
2003	41
Grand total	20,589

M6 (E63-64)

Model name and code

M6, E63/64

Claim to fame

V-10-powered, fast, frantic, and complicated; more an engineering milestone than a GT to enjoy

Years in production

2004–2010

Number built

14,152

Launch price

£83,300 (€116,000)

Engine code and type

S85 B50, 90-degree V-10, DOHC 40-valve, variable valve timing, Siemens engine management

Displacement, cc

4,999

Peak power hp @ rpm

507@7,750

Max torque, Nm @ rpm

520@6,100

Transmission and drive

7-speed SMG III sequential, rear; DSC and M Variable Differential Lock

Alternative transmission

6-speed manual (North America only)

Suspension, front

MacPherson struts, lower wishbones

Suspension, rear

Multilink system with twin transverse links, trailing arms, tie bars, coils

Body styles

Two-door coupé and convertible

Curb weight, kg

1,710

Max speed (km/h) and 1–100 km/h (sec)

250 (restricted)/305; 4.6

Production by year

2010	405
2009	494
2008	2,016
2007	3,882
2006	5,175
2005	2,138
2004	42
Grand total	14,152

M3 (E90)

Model name and code

M3, E90/92/93

Claim to fame

Fourth-gen M3 used high-revving V-8 for stunning speed but lacked the magic of its straight six predecessor

Years in production

2006–2013

Number built

65,985

Launch price

£51,000 (€74,000)

Engine code and type

S65 B40, 90-degree V-8, DOHC 32-valve, variable valve timing

Displacement, cc

3,999

Peak power hp @ rpm

420@8,300

Max torque, Nm @ rpm

400@3,900

Transmission and drive

7-speed M-DCT dual-clutch automatic/sequential, rear, DSC

Alternative transmission

6-speed manual

Suspension, front

MacPherson struts, forged alloy lower wishbones

Suspension, rear

Multilink axle with trailing arms, transverse links, lower control arms, coils

Body styles

Two-door coupé and convertible; four-door sedan

Curb weight, kg

1,580 (coupé)

Max speed (km/h) and 1–100 km/h (sec)

250; 4.8 (manual), 4.6 (M-DCT)

Production by year

2013	3,776
2012	6,160
2011	10,543
2010	10,553
2009	8,524
2008	20,151
2007	6,215
2006	63
Grand total	65,985

EXCURSION
OFF-ROAD
THE M SUVs

8

Contentious at
first, the hotshot
X5M and X6M
soon won the
world over

Launching in 2009, the X6M
and X5M opened up a whole
new area of the premium
market—the segment
for high-performance
heavyweight SUVs.

M VERSIONS OF BMW'S X series of SUVs and crossovers have remained acutely controversial for many years, but that notoriety stems from more than just the aftershocks of contentious styling decisions, as was the case with the first-generation X6 in 2008.

At the root of all the early fuss was the notion, hard-wired into the psyche of any BMW enthusiast or commentator in the 1990s, that their beloved brand must not even *consider* developing an off-road model. The very real fear was that adding a heavy and unresponsive vehicle to the lineup risked forever torpedoing BMW's carefully nurtured status as the "ultimate driving machine." To take the doubters' argument further, gracing such a palpably discordant monstrosity with the super-exclusive M badge would be to add insult to injury. How, the sceptics asked, could something related to a truck possibly be reconciled with the racetrack heritage that had always been written into M Division's ethos?

To understand those questions, we need to go back a decade or more before the appearance of the first X5M—to the 1990s, in fact, and to the different set of values that prevailed at the time. It had been clear to BMW for some time that the company needed to expand its production numbers to realize the economies of scale necessary to compete profitably in global markets. That expansion, company managers reasoned, could best be achieved through the annexation of additional market sectors, if necessary employing other brand names to maintain the exclusivity of the core BMW marque.

BMW bought the Rover Group in 1994 mainly to gain access to Land Rover's expertise in 4x4s. Disappointment with the outdated technologies it found prompted BMW to develop its own SUV designs.

Cash-rich and acquisitive under its new CEO, Bernd Pischetsrieder, BMW stunned the word in January 1994 by scooping up Britain's Rover group, which included Land Rover. The famous 4x4 marque was regarded as the most glittering prize of all, a premium brand ideally placed to exploit the fast-rising sales graph of sport utility vehicles in the US.

But all was not what it seemed: Land Rover was a much tougher nut to crack than BMW had anticipated. Most Land Rover models, even the luxury Range Rover, were shockingly outdated by BMW standards. It became clear that time- and budget-consuming re-engineering from the ground up would be needed to reach acceptable standards of dynamics.

In the interim, BMW began exploring some of Land Rover's proprietary technologies. These included its clever Hill Descent Control, which used the vehicle's ABS sensors to achieve easily controllable crawling speeds down steep and slippery slopes without the driver having to touch the brakes or select an ultralow gear. Intrigued by what he found in Land Rover's technical toolbox, Dr. Wolfgang Reitzle, BMW's powerful engineering chief, was impatient to explore the possibilities of sharing technologies between the brands. "We would love to see what a BMW Land Rover would look like," he told designer Frank Stephenson, who recalls that this quickly escalated into a command to produce a full-size styling model within six weeks, a near-impossible schedule.

Famously, Stephenson sketched the concept for what turned out to be the X5 on a two-hour flight to a business meeting. Borrowing the platform from the 5-Series sedan, he raised the ride height and passenger cabin considerably, added large wheels with chunky tires, and beefed up the familiar BMW design features to provide a more imposing look. The effect, which came as a shock at the time, was that of a 5-Series Touring that had taken a large dose of steroids, though to everyone's relief the macho image stopped well short of the slablike trucks that filled American producers with such pride. Underneath the elevated body were largely 5-Series mechanicals, including the four-wheel-drive system codeveloped with Steyr for the Touring, plus air suspension units to provide adjustable ride height for off-road conditions. Power was provided by the 4.4-liter V-8 from the 7-Series.

▼ The first-generation X5 revolutionized perceptions of SUV ride, steering, and handling when it appeared in 1999. Its strong dynamics led BMW to fit larger and more powerful engines.

▲ Frank Stephenson famously sketched the original X5 on a flight to a meeting. He is best known for his first-generation BMW Mini and his work at McLaren.

Many at the time felt the macho image of the coupé-style X6M to be too aggressive for a BMW, but there was no denying that the M engineers had been highly successful in making a two-ton SUV accelerate and corner like a sports sedan; the X5M was equally fast but attracted less criticism.

Equally important, however, was what BMW left off its shopping list for the X5. Firmly rejected was the weighty and twist-prone body-on-chassis construction then still de rigueur in the 4x4 world. In its place, the X5 offered the taut unitary structure of a luxury car. Out, too, were the clunky transfer gearbox and diff-locks beloved by the off-road fraternity; the heavy, truck-style rigid axles were junked in favor of long-travel independent suspension all round.

All this gave credibility to BMW's assertion, prior to the reveal in January 1999, that the X5 was a new type of product—an SAV, or sports *activity* vehicle—in contrast to the truck-like SUVs that people were familiar with and whose dynamic limitations were well recognized. Crucially, BMW had realized that most SUV buyers weren't interested in extreme Jeep-style off-road capability and that they were choosing the 4x4 format mainly for its high driving position and chunky, macho image. The dreadful on-road behavior of the standard SUV was simply regarded as a price that had to be paid.

Today, two decades down the road, it's easy to regard that first X5 as simply another SUV. But as the first SUV that was actually decent to drive in town, on the highway, and on motorways, the X5 was a genuine breakthrough design whose impact was immense. Here was a 4x4 that steered straight and precise, rather than wandering vaguely; it wasn't scary to drive fast as it turned crisply into bends, and it didn't feel like it was about to tip over. What's more, it didn't kick about on bad roads or sway alarmingly in side winds, and it pulled up confidently under heavy braking.

In short, it was the first of its genre to drive as well as a good car—and this is what gave BMW M GmbH engineers the confidence to develop a series of sports versions with ever-higher levels of performance.

Inventing the Performance SUV: X5M (E70) and X6M (E71)

The enthusiastic customer reception given the original E53 X5 in its first years on the market encouraged BMW to broaden its appeal, enlarge its engine by stages to 4.8 liters and 360 horsepower, and add more electronic control to its 4WD drivetrain. Already there had been something of a diversion in the shape of an insane one-off—a Motorsport-engineered X5 that, despite looking nearly standard, crammed BMW's Le Mans–winning V-12 under the hood: with 700 horsepower on tap it had lapped the Nürburgring in under 7 minutes and 50 seconds. With so much power it was widely seen as a no more than a clever publicity stunt; little did people realize that, within less than two short decades, a standard showroom X5M would be offering very nearly as much horsepower.

BMW soon complemented the E53 X5 with the smaller X3, launched in 2003, but before long the newcomer was snapping at its bigger brother's heels and it was time for a second-generation X5. In 2006 the notably larger E70 duly appeared, the swollen dimensions making space for the optional third row of seats craved by US customers. Again, despite its bulk, the new car drove well for an SUV, dispelling any lingering doubts about BMW's entry into this lucrative sector.

Drawn by BMW's success, however, others were beginning to catch up—most notably Porsche, whose Cayenne gave an even sportier slant on the SUV theme, threatening to make the X5 seem a tad staid and to cream off some of BMW's top-end customers. Cue the X6, whose 2008 launch stirred up a hornet's nest of comment, some favorable but most of it furious.

Most definitely a one-off: the special X5 Le Mans crammed the V-12 engine from BMW's 24-Hours-winning prototype under its hood, resulting in a Nürburgring lap time of 7 minutes 50 seconds. By 2020 the standard production X5M and X6M would be approaching the V-12's 700-horsepower power output.

With the X6, BMW claimed to have invented an entirely new vehicle segment, that of the SAC, or sports activity *coupé*. Though mechanically and structurally similar to the X5, the X6's cutdown roofline and fastback rear tailgate gave it a really menacing, predatory look, emphasizing the muscularity of the underbody, the vastness of the wheels and tires, the dominating height of the bodysides, and, especially, the towering rear end. It drove even better than the standard X5; if there was any X model crying out for the M treatment, the X6 was it. And to add to the sense of urgency, the rival Cayenne had just burst through the 500-horsepower barrier and Mercedes's second-generation ML-class was spawning a 6.3-liter AMG sports version boasting 510 horsepower.

Thus the 2009 New York motor show played host to not one but two M-Model debuts—the X5M and the X6M. Externally, the M GmbH engineers specified typically subtle enhancements, such as a deeper front fascia incorporating even larger air intakes, and a revised rear bumper assembly housing the quadruple exhaust tailpipes, made more intimidating in the X6M thanks to its jacked-up tail. Though all X5s and X6s have always been assembled in Spartanburg, North Carolina, the complete M-specification drivetrains were always shipped over from Germany. Under the skin, as befits any M model, the upgrades were more extensive, and the X5M and X6M pairing signaled many important firsts both for M GmbH and the broader BMW group. These were the first M models to incorporate four-wheel drive, the first with automatic-only transmissions, the first with torque vectoring on the rear axle, and, historically, the first BMWs since the 1974 2002 Turbo to feature turbocharged engines. M Division made less of a fuss about the fact that these were also the first M models to tip the scales at over two tons: in fact, the lofty X5M, laden with luxury equipment, topped out at almost 2.4 tons.

At least part of that weight increase must have been due to the substantial engineering input delivered by the M GmbH specialists in their mission to turn a tall and bulky 4x4 into a proper performance machine. The S63B44 V-8 engine, while retaining the 4.4-liter capacity of the all-alloy N53 from the standard car, broke new ground for both BMW and the whole auto industry with its "hot" twin-turbo layout. Instead of mounting the exhaust manifolds and turbos on the outside of each bank of cylinders, BMW located them inside the vee: the advantages realized included more compact packaging and reduced weight but also improved engine performance as the cylinders' exhaust pulses combined to keep the two turbos spinning faster at lower engine rpm. Now with a 6,800 rpm rev limit, the S63 delivered no less than 555 horsepower at 6,000 rpm, along with a whopping 680 Nm of torque all the way from 1,500 to 5,650 rpm.

That huge Porsche-baiting energy was fed through a beefed-up six-speed ZF automatic with electronically controlled distribution of torque to all four wheels. On the rear axle was a further innovation: a torque vectoring differential that could feed extra power to the outside rear wheel under cornering, enhancing yaw response and minimizing any tendency to understeer. The M specification already sent more of the power to the rear than on standard X5s and X6s; this could be further increased by switching to M-Dynamic mode, which also raised the threshold at which the stability control systems intervened. On the suspension side, the mountings and bushings were stiffened, the air springs firmed up, and the Active Roll Stabilization system, first seen in the 7-Series, recalibrated for flatter cornering.

The effect was remarkable, especially in the X6M with its more coupé-like feel from behind the wheel. Here was a big, bullying vehicle where you had to climb up into the driver's seat, where there was huge acceleration as you surfed the tidal wave of torque with the slightest brush of the throttle pedal; here was quick and responsive steering that totally belied the monster's great height and two-ton mass. And, at the end of a long drive in what felt like a muscular sports car, you'd be surprised to open the driver's door and drop a long way to the ground, so easy was it to forget that this was a high-riding SUV.

The 4.4-liter V-8 in the X5M and X6M broke new engineering ground with its "hot-vee" placement of the twin turbochargers between the two banks of cylinders. This gave quicker throttle pick-up and a substantial 555 horsepower— enough to launch the models to 100 km/h in 4.7 seconds.

The interiors of both models were every bit as luxurious as BMW's top-end business sedans, and Active Roll Stabilization technology helped improve comfort by reducing body lean under cornering. Six-speed automatic transmission was standard across the lineup.

For BMW M, this was mission accomplished. Though there were many commentators who still harbored misgivings about the very concept of a high-performance SUV, the X5M and X6M had demonstrated with genuine panache that such a machine was indeed possible and, even more importantly, that it could be exciting and rewarding to drive. It worked for a variety of reasons beyond those of its prodigious performance: M engineers had succeeded in giving it the quick steering essential to any sporty car, and the M-Dynamic electronics allowed the driver a true personalization of the driving experience. At least in the case of the X5M, it was probably the only vehicle in the world capable of seating seven—and hitting 100 kilometers per hour in under 4.7 seconds.

Did these M models ever venture off-road for a spot of mud wrestling or Jeep-style boulder crawling? And do they still stand up as genuinely credible M Cars alongside the core M3 and M5 nameplates? Hand on heart, the answers to all three are probably negative, though no doubt some examples have seen service hauling trailers with jet skis or classic motorcycles aboard. A few may have even taken part in the occasional track day session. On the positive side, the M GmbH engineers had made their point decisively and convincingly: in defiance of established engineering wisdom, a big, heavy, spacious SUV can indeed be made to go, handle, and corner nearly as well as a hotshot sports sedan—even if it might be somewhat less subtle in the process.

Launched in 2009, the first X5M opened up a new market segment for high-performance heavyweight 4x4s. Its X6M coupé sibling stirred up controversy with its more aggressive style, but both now seem tame in comparison with the excesses of later generations of power SUVs.

X5M & X6M (E70-71)

Model name and code	
X5M, E70	X6M, E71

Claim to fame	
The original hot SUV; high powered, fast, and agile despite its weight; showed M's skill in making bulky 4x4s feel sporty	Shock coupé styling sparked global trend for aggressive, overpowered SUVs; performance is beyond question

Years in production	
2008–2013	2008–2014

Number built	
8,794	10,678

Launch price	
£90,000	£93,000

Engine code and type	
S33B44, 90-degree V-8, twin OHC per bank, double VANOS variable valve timing, twin turbo	S33B44, 90-degree V-8, twin OHC per bank, double VANOS variable valve timing, twin turbo

Displacement, cc	
4,395	4,395

Peak power hp @ rpm	
555@6,000	555@6,000

Max torque, Nm @ rpm	
680@1,500–5,650	680@1,500–5,650

Transmission and drive	
6-speed automatic, permanent AWD, variable torque split, torque vectoring rear differential	6-speed automatic, permanent AWD, variable torque split, torque vectoring rear differential

Suspension, front	
Double wishbones and coil-spring/damper units	Double wishbones and coil-spring/damper units

Suspension, rear	
Multilink axle, coil springs, self-leveling, active roll stabilization	Multilink axle, coil springs, self-leveling, active roll stabilization

Body styles	
Five-door SUV	Five-door SUV

Curb weight, kg	
2,305	2,305

Max speed (km/h) and 1–100 km/h (sec)	
250 (restricted)/275; 4.7	250 (restricted)/275; 4.7

Production by year			
2013	441	2014	403
2012	1,647	2013	1,314
2011	2,387	2012	1,548
2010	2,456	2011	2,683
2009	2,027	2010	2,599
2008	16	2009	2,120
Grand total	8,974	2008	11
		Grand total	10,678

For a key to specification tables, see page 221

THE 2010s

FIRST-GENERATION TURBOS—
M TAKES A CHANCE

9

From the wild
1M Coupé via
the svelte M5
to the fast and
furious M4 GTS

The F80-82 marked the split
into dual names—M4 for
Coupés and M3 for sedans—
and, more controversially, it
introduced turbocharging.
Here, a 2014 M4 poses on the
finishing straight in front of
its iconic M3 forebears—E30,
E36, E46, and E90.

IT IS SEPTEMBER 2008 and the collapse of the Lehman Brothers investment bank goes down as the biggest failure in corporate history. This directly triggers the worldwide financial crisis of 2008–2009, tipping countless businesses into bankruptcy, prompting rapid changes to financial regulations and a rethink in boardrooms on how to do business.

Gone was the boom-era mantra that greed is good. Conspicuous displays of extravagance and wealth suddenly seemed out of place, and sales stuttered as consumption crumbled. But while both General Motors and Chrysler were caught off-guard and later filed for Chapter 11 bankruptcy, BMW was better prepared than most. The far-reaching strategic review it had carried out the year before had included several scenario planning exercises, one of which projected a contingency in the event of a sudden collapse in demand. Ian Robertson, board member for global sales and marketing at the time, vividly recalls the position:

> I can remember a very important discussion we had at the Paris auto show in October 2008, when I was looking at our monthly figures for September that year. They were coming through on my BlackBerry (which is what I was using at the time) and they were minus 30, minus 35, minus 40 percent—and it was everywhere. I said to CEO Norbert Reithofer, "There's something very serious happening out there, and whilst I'm not sure how it will develop, we need to review our forward plans."

Robertson and the BMW board took the brave decision to take seventy-eight thousand cars out of the production schedule before Christmas. This helped the company come out of that year with its cash flow in much better shape than its rivals. Through this swift action BMW was able to avoid the short- and medium-term crises that engulfed those around it. It was also clear that customers' priorities were shifting, to which BMW responded by doing more than slowing the production tempo: the whole portfolio of future products was reexamined in context of the downturn.

Wanton extravagance would no longer be welcome in the new, post-crisis era, reasoned the BMW planners. One public consequence of this new thinking was the cancellation of the flagship Grand Turismo GT project, based on the extravagant CS prototype shown in 2007—and within the M GmbH division there were important aftershocks too. When it came to the staple M3 and M5 model lines, for instance, it was apparent to all that the race for more and more cylinders, higher revs, and ever more engineering complexity would have to end. The M3 had started life with four cylinders and now boasted eight; the M5 had swelled from six, through eight, to its present ten. Though mechanically appealing and searingly powerful, the prodigious fuel thirst of these intricate engines marked them as out of sync with the new, more efficiency-conscious era that was dawning.

Mindful of M Division's ground rule that each new M-Car generation must offer better performance than the outgoing model, the BMW engineers knew that there was only one way to improve both power and efficiency—by moving to turbocharging. This led in turn to a whole new way of thinking about how M-developed cars would drive, how they would respond, and, most critically for many enthusiasts, what they would sound like.

E82 1-Series M Coupé:
Entry-Level Wild Child Reconnects with M's Roots

The unchecked engineering escalation that characterized the core M3 and M5 models in the 2000s had led to the growing realization that M GmbH's products were in danger of losing touch with their roots, in particular the spirit of compact but still thrilling first-generation M3, with under 200 horsepower. BMW feared that customers who wanted the raw fun of sports car driving might switch to simple hot hatchbacks instead of their complex and technologically super-sophisticated M models.

What was needed was an accessible entry-level model that replicated the playful, fun element of the original M3, albeit in a modern context, taking into account the multitude of safety and emission-control rules that had sprung up in the intervening quarter century. Enter, first, the 135i. The five-door 1-Series hatchback had been launched in 2004 with a selection of four-cylinder engines; 3.0-liter six-cylinder versions joined the range in 2007, with the top 135i adding turbocharging to deliver 302 horsepower. In addition, BMW used the 2007 Tokyo show to unveil a tii Concept design study. Its stubby two-door styling drew critical comments and no engineering details were given, but the study did prompt speculation about a future M version of the 1-Series.

Power pack: the 1-Series M Coupé was an M Car in nearly every detail and combined the chunky Coupé body with M3 suspension and a highly potent straight six turbo engine to make it BMW M Division's first turbocharged sports car. The results were predictably spectacular.

▲ ◥◥ Steroid injection: 1-Series M Coupé was brash and assertive, from its swollen wheelarches and broad tires to the outrageous power of the N54 turbo engine that made it the wild child of the BMW family.

Yet when the new model finally did appear in 2011, its chunky looks came across as almost as awkward as its 1-Series M Coupé name, chosen to avoid any clash with the near-sacred M1 of 1978. Many were reminded of the equally ungainly—and divisive—Z3-based M Coupé of 1998: both had unconventional proportions and had, by all accounts, been developed against a compressed timetable. In particular, the 1's truncated rear, aggressive front and rear aprons, blistered wheelarches, and wide-set wheels gave it the look of a pumped-up tuner car.

But when it came to the 1M Coupé's technical specification, there could be no argument. Its shortened proportions gave it a footprint similar to the original M3's; its suspension, steering, and braking systems were taken straight from the then-current E90 M3; and the 3.0-liter N54 straight six engine boasted twin turbochargers. This gave the 1M Coupé the perhaps dubious honor of being M's first turbocharged sports car, though the V-8 turbo X5M and X6M SUVs had appeared the year before. Strictly speaking, the N54 engine was not a Motorsport development, but the M engineers' work on the software and boost and exhaust systems resulted in a useful increase in power to 340 horsepower and more amenable torque characteristics than a highly tuned nonturbo motor would have had.

Nevertheless, that amount of power and torque in such a small, short-wheelbase car demanded a lot of care and restraint from the driver. In the interest of simplification, BMW had dispensed with many of the complicated electronic control systems of the M3 and M5, leaving only the Variable M Differential Lock and the DSC, whose intervention thresholds could be raised by selecting M-Dynamic mode on the steering wheel M button. That setting was fine for experienced drivers on a track day, but for normal customers on public roads it made the Coupé quite a handful, especially in wet conditions; this served only to further polarize opinion.

◀ Twin turbos on the N54 straight six made the 1-Series M Coupé BMW's first turbocharged sports car. The engine was not officially a Motorsport development but benefited from M expertise in its software and boost control.

Magazine road testers loved its lurid, tail-sliding driftability and its easy surges of acceleration. Others, however, found it too old school and unsubtle—a car let down by its boy-racer image, compromised accommodation, and comparatively high price. Though the consensus was that the 1-Series M Coupé did just about qualify as a proper M Car, fewer than sixty-four hundred were built over its barely eighteen-month production life. But, as always with BMW, important lessons had been learned.

As M's first stab at a return to its M3 roots, the 1-Series M Coupé might have been a disappointment, but the models that succeeded it were dramatically better—most especially the "pure-blooded" M2 CS that, as we will see in the following chapter, proved to be an absolute belter.

Revs and Cylinders Give Way to Turbo Boost: F10 M5 Makes the Big Shift

The fifth generation of the M5, which debuted in late 2011, marks the crucial tipping point when hard-line M enthusiasts—those subscribing to the core M3 and M5 lines—finally came up against the harsh reality that their favorite cars could no longer keep on getting bigger, more complex, and more wasteful.

So while the outgoing E60 M5 had a race-bred 5-liter V-10 engine screaming to almost 8,500 rpm, its replacement made do with just eight cylinders and 4.4 liters. In place of the quirky, Bangle-inspired style of the old car came a calmer and more measured look, with BMW grilles that were larger and more upright. The new vehicle carried on M Division's maxim of always improving on the outgoing product and, despite its subtler allure, this M5 succeeded in packing an even bigger punch and racking up even better figures than its forebear.

The secret was down to that single word the purists had been dreading for a long time: turbocharging. Many saw the turbocharger as the lazy way to bolt on extra power. Others were worried that the turbo engines would suffer from lag at low rpm and run out of puff at the top end, while many more feared the move to turbos would result in a sanitized product that did not feel or sound like a true M Car. In the event, however, only the last of those fears was realized, and one of the principal complaints

All change: the F10-generation M5 displayed a much sharper style than its Bangle-shaped predecessor, but the main talking point was its turbo V-8 engine, the first in any core M Car.

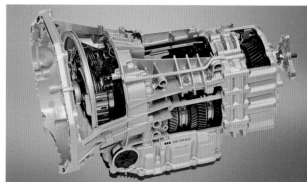

leveled against the F10 version was that of the synthesized engine noise that BMW fed into the car's audio speakers to make up for the lack of induction noise from the turbocharged engine.

By way of assuaging those fears around big turbos, BMW M engineers could already point to two years of experience with the potent hot-V twin-turbo V-8 in the X5M and X6M. Indeed, it was precisely this S63B44 unit that formed the basis for the new M5 powerplant. For its new application, though, the engine had to go one better, with M engineers now adding Valvetronic valve control, fitting larger twin-scroll turbochargers, and raising both the static compression ratio and the boost pressure. The outcome was a dramatic 560 horsepower from 5,000 to 6,000 rpm; later Competition versions would give 575 or even a full 600 horsepower. But the most remarkable difference was in the torque characteristics: the new engine produced over 675 Nm all the way from 1,500 to 5,750 rpm. This was 30 percent more than the V-10's and, more to the point, it was usable right through the rev range rather than peaking sharply at over 6,000 rpm.

The seven-speed dual-clutch M-DCT transmission from the E90 M3 was a welcome replacement for the unpopular SMG III of the E60 M5; as before, a six-speed manual was an option in North America only. The transmission modes were simplified from eleven to six, and a rather less daunting array of optional settings for the Dynamic Stability Control and Active M differential were again made more accessible through two customizable M modes via steering wheel buttons.

The twin-turbo V-8's 560 horsepower ensured the F10 M5 comfortably out-accelerated its high-revving V-10 predecessor, but without the noise or the drama—much to the chagrin of enthusiasts. Later versions would nudge the 600 horsepower barrier. The multi-mode seven-speed M-DCT dual-clutch transmission was a major improvement over the unloved SMG III of the previous M5, and even the Active M differential could be fine-tuned by the driver.

The F10 M5 outperformed its predecessor on every objective measure and had a suite of electronic chassis and driveline control systems that drivers could tailor to their own preferences through the central iDrive controller.

The chassis preserved the layout and basic principles of the standard car but specially developed M suspension components strengthened and stiffened the setup and fine-tuned its geometry for sharper handling. The brakes were similarly upgraded to six-pot calipers up front, with carbon ceramic rotors available a year into the production run; the 19-inch wheels had 9-inch rims at the front and 10-inch ones at the rear. Bodywork enhancements were typically low key, with a unique front fascia that substituted the standard foglights for extra air intakes. The front fenders were widened and carried discreet inset M5-insignia air exit grilles, and the rear bumper was reshaped to carry the familiar quad exhaust outlets.

On the road, the new M5 was as easy to drive as its predecessor was tricky. For a big car it was remarkably agile, disguising its increased weight effectively and riding with convincing smoothness and body control on the softest of its three suspension settings. The engine responded to the throttle as quickly as anyone could wish for and the dual-clutch transmission was cooperative rather than jerky and obstructive. As for outright performance, it had loads: the V-8 turbo was even quicker than the V-10, hitting 100 kilometers per hour in 4.4 seconds, and, even though the engine would rev beyond 7,200 rpm, there was no need to use such extreme speeds.

So where, then, was the problem—apart from the price, which had shot up to near six figures in dollar markets? Different commentators summed it up in different ways, but the clearest common thread was the sentiment that this new M5 did not stir the emotions in the same unmistakable way as its predecessor. The sense of drama was gone, the intimidation factor had been stifled, there was no bloodcurdling scream at peak revs, and it was embarrassingly easy to drive. In short, as one magazine put it, the new car was faster, cleaner, and more efficient—but also less flawed and less fun.

Everything Changes as F80-82 M3 and M4 Go Turbo and Nameplates Split

As with the larger M5, everything changed for this, the fifth generation of the M3. Even the name changed, for from 2013 what had been known as the 3-Series split into two separate model lines and the version of greatest interest to enthusiasts, the Coupé, became the new 4-Series. Sedans, Touring station wagons, and a new Gran Turismo hatchback variant retained the 3-Series badging, though in engineering terms the two divergent series were nearly identical.

All this meant that it was the four-door M3 sedan that was the first to arrive as a 2014 model-year car carrying the internal F80 coding. The Coupé M4, designated F82, arrived in spring 2014 and the F83 M4 Convertible later that year. All three closely followed the tauter, crisper new look of their parent models, and though the open car retained the rigid folding hardtop roof principle of its predecessor, the roofline was much less awkward and the style more akin to that of a fabric soft-top.

In terms of external upgrades, the new M3/M4 models followed the familiar M pattern of a reshaped hood and wider front fenders, all in aluminum, with larger frontal air intakes—especially the deep central one—and an enlarged rear diffuser structure accommodating the quadruple exhaust outlets. But as always, the engineering

Leading the charge: M Division's highest profile sports coupé gained a new name, M4, and a turbocharged engine for 2014. Power, speed, and dynamics were all improved, but that was not enough to convince some hard-core M fans.

The M4 Convertible made a fabulous—if pricey—four-seater sports car. It retained the rigid metal folding roof of the previous generation, but the roof-up silhouette was more attractive.

specifications were the most important, and here it was the new straight six S55 engine that clearly led the way. Described by BMW as a high-revving 3-liter with specially developed M TwinTurbo technology, the S55 gave 431 horsepower between 5,500 and 7,300 rpm and was redlined at 7,600.

The twin single-scroll turbos materially aided throttle response at all speeds, as evidenced by the 550 Nm torque all the way from 1,850 to 5,500 rpm—a 40 percent increase over the outgoing V-8. With all-up weight reduced by some 80 kilograms, fuel consumption and emissions dropped by a quarter and the 0–100 kilometer-per-hour acceleration time was trimmed to just 4.3 seconds in the manual model, or 4.1 with the M-DCT.

Inside the engine there was a lighter and stiffer forged crankshaft, sprayed-on coatings instead of conventional cylinder liners, and a magnesium sump with extra baffles and oil pumps to guarantee lubrication under sustained lateral g during track driving. The high and low temperature cooling circuits took on greater complexity, incorporating charge air cooling, a main engine radiator, oil coolers for both engine and transmission, and an extra electric pump to keep the turbocharger cool when stationary.

The six-speed manual transmission now incorporated automatic throttle blips when downshifting, and the third-generation seven-speed M-DCT included launch control and a stability mechanism that opened the clutches to bring the car back into line if cornering understeer became excessive. Further complementing the sophisticated specification were a carbon propshaft, which allowed the center bearing to be dispensed with, the Active M differential giving progressive lock from 0 to 100 percent, and an advanced lightweight suspension system with stiffer spring rates. The steering, finally, moved to electrohydraulic assistance—the first time M Division had departed from fully hydraulic—giving the driver the choice of three different settings.

Industrially, too, there were important differences. While the sedan M3 was built at Regensburg, the M4 Coupé and Convertible returned to BMW's core Preussenstrasse plant, twenty-three years after it last made M Cars.

While the turbo-generation M5 had been launched to less than wholehearted praise from magazine commentators, the M3 and M4 fared somewhat better—though still short of the ecstatic reception given to the E46 more than a decade earlier. Yes, there were grumbles that the new turbo M3 and M4 didn't sound as throaty or as inspiring as the outgoing V-8, except at peak revs; and the extra torque meant the engine didn't have to be worked half as hard, thus diluting the sense of driver involvement. But overall, there was grudging praise for almost every other aspect of the new generation's performance—from the remarkable acceleration to the impressive throttle response, the range of steering, suspension, and transmission settings, and the hugely effective (though optional at considerable extra cost) carbon ceramic brakes.

If there was a caveat, so the consensus went, it was that, while the new M4 (and by implication the M3 as well) was more competent on an objective level than its predecessor, this did not necessarily make it any more enjoyable to drive. More than anything, said one commentator, "I want a little more feel and interaction from my M3/M4."

Turbocharging gave the M3 and M4's high-revving 3-liter straight six an easy 431 horsepower as well as torque 40 percent greater than the outgoing V-8. Note the substantial cross-bracing in the engine bay. Both the M4 Coupé and the M3 sedan (pictured) were deceptively fast, if lacking in driver engagement.

Complaints like these were addressed in sometimes spectacular fashion by the series of special editions that soon followed. The Competition Package version boasted a dozen extra horsepower and revised suspension settings for tauter handling, but the 2017 CS, for Competition Sport, went one further, rising to 454 horsepower with an additional 50 Nm of torque thanks to recalibrated engine software. Carbon fiber components such as seat shells and door liners helped trim the mass by some 35 kilograms, allowing 100 kilometers per hour to appear in under 4 seconds and the maximum speed to top out at 280 kilometers per hour. Adding to the aural excitement were exhaust crackles on the overrun. Contemporary accounts speak of the prodigious grip and improved steering response attributable to the Michelin Pilot Sport tires—but they also warn of the need to exercise care in the rain.

For all its excesses, though, the CS was not the most extreme expression of the M4 theme. That honor was reserved for the M4 GTS, a barely disguised racer for the road. A full 70 kilograms lighter still, it sported a race-style, full-width aerodynamic wing

The 2017 M4 GTS was one of the most extreme road cars ever produced by M Division, with lowered and stiffened suspension, race-style spoiler and roll cage, and novel water injection boosting its engine to 500 horsepower. Harsh and sensitive on ordinary roads, it made a much better track weapon.

perched on the rear deck lid. It had huge gold wheels, too, and the roll cage that replaced the rear seats was also finished in gold. Subtle it was not—but those who accused it of visual grandstanding were swiftly silenced by a glance at its engine specification: the GTS was the first production car in the world to feature water injection (into the manifold) to further boost its power under peak load.

The resultant 500 horsepower tire-smoked the GTS to 100 kilometers per hour in under 3.8 seconds and pushed its top speed well past the landmark 300 kilometer-per-hour threshold. Released in a limited edition of just seven hundred units, it quickly sold out despite a prodigious price of €146,000—more than double that of the standard car. The fortunate few who have driven it report a highly involving and extremely responsive car, but also one that was high strung, nervous, and uncharacteristically raw and hard-edged for a BMW. The consensus was that the GTS might be better suited to the racetrack than the road, particularly in poor conditions. Echoes of the original 2002 Turbo, perhaps?

1M Coupé (F82)

Model name and code	
1M Coupé, F82	
Claim to fame	
Oddball entry-level coupé overdosed on power for crazy handling that got even crazier in wet conditions	
Years in production	
2011–2012	
Number built	
6,342	
Launch price	
£40,000 (€48,200)	
Engine code and type	
N54, straight six, DOHC 24-valve, twin turbo	
Displacement, cc	
2,979	
Peak power hp @ rpm	
340@5,900	
Max torque, Nm @ rpm	
500@1,500–4,500	
Transmission and drive	
6-speed manual, rear	
Suspension, front	
MacPherson struts with lower wishbones and lateral control arms	
Suspension, rear	
Multilink with coil springs, control arms	
Body styles	
Two-door coupé	
Curb weight, kg	
1,495	
Max speed (km/h) and 1–100 km/h (sec)	
250; 4.9	

Production by year

2012	2,158
2011	4,151
2010	33
Grand total	6,342

M5 (F10)

Model name and code	
M5, F10	
Claim to fame	
Twin-turbo V-8 gave even more power and speed than outgoing V-10, but lack of aural drama was a letdown	
Years in production	
2010–2016	
Number built	
19,533	
Launch price	
£73,040 (€88,000)	
Engine code and type	
S63 B44TO, 90-degree V-8, 32-valve, twin OHC per bank, Valvetronic, twin turbo	
Displacement, cc	
4,395	
Peak power hp @ rpm	
560@6,000–7,000	
Max torque, Nm @ rpm	
680@1,500–5,750	
Transmission and drive	
7-speed M-DCT dual-clutch automatic, rear axle with Active M differential	
Alternative transmission	
6-speed manual (North America only)	
Suspension, front	
Double wishbones with lateral links, coil spring damper units and electronic dampers	
Suspension, rear	
Integral multilink with coil springs and electronic dampers	
Body styles	
Four-door sedan	
Curb weight, kg	
1,870	
Max speed (km/h) and 1–100 km/h (sec)	
250 (305 with optional M Driver's Pack); 4.4	

Production by year

2016	1,292
2015	2,266
2014	3,050
2013	4,516
2012	7,122
2011	1,244
2010	43
Grand total	19,533

For a key to specification tables, see page 221

M3 & M4 (F80-82)

Model name and code	
M3, F80	M4, F82

Claim to fame	
Fifth-gen M3 reverts to high-revving straight six; deceptively fast, if lacking in driver engagement	Coupé and Convertible get new M4 nameplate and different styling; like M3, very rapid and capable but short on communication

Years in production	
2012–2018	2013–2020

Number built	
34,677	77,624

Launch price	
£59,900 (€72,100)	€73,200 (Convertible)

Engine code and type	
S55B30TO, straight six, DOHC 24-valve, Valvetronic, twin turbochargers	S55B30TO, straight six, DOHC 24-valve, Valvetronic, twin turbochargers

Displacement, cc	
2,979	2,979

Peak power hp @ rpm	
431@5,500–7,300	431@5,500–7,300

Max torque, Nm @ rpm	
550@1,850–5,500	550@1,850–5,500

Transmission and drive	
6-speed manual, rear wheels, Active M differential	6-speed manual, rear wheels, Active M differential

Alternative transmission	
7-speed M-DCT dual-clutch automatic	7-speed M-DCT dual-clutch automatic

Suspension, front	
Double wishbones, coli spring damper units, control arms	Double wishbones, coli spring damper units, control arms

Suspension, rear	
Five-link axle, control arms, coil springs	Five-link axle, control arms, coil springs

Body styles	
Four-door sedan	Two-door coupé and convertible

Curb weight, kg	
1,537	1,497 (M4 Coupé); 1750 (Convertible)

Max speed (km/h) and 1–100 km/h (sec)	
250; 4.3 (4.1 with M-DCT)	250; 4.3 (4.1 with M-DCT), 4.6/4.4 (Convertible)

Production by year			
2018	6,862	2020	2,272
2017	8,149	2019	7,851
2016	8,428	2018	10,166
2015	6,625	2017	14,439
2014	4,470	2016	13,437
2013	92	2015	14,899
2012	51	2014	14,429
Grand total	34,677	2013	131
		Grand total	77,624

THE 2020s

M2, M3, M4, M5—
TURBOCHARGED TO PERFECTION

Back in top form with spectacular
speed and driver appeal

10

Compact, agile, and
bursting with power,
the M2 represented
a welcome return to
M's original ethos
of intense driver
engagement.

ONCE, IN AN INTERVIEW I remember well, I spoke at length to Honda's racing supremo Nobuhiko Kawamoto, the brains behind the Japanese company's string of Formula 1 successes in the 1980s and later the CEO of the whole organization. He revealed that he learned more about engine development when the Honda racing team was losing than when they were winning. So how does that apply to BMW M GmbH, whose failures or even near misses are so few and far between that they're hardly worth citing?

Rewind to the mid-2000s and the dilemma faced by the designers and builders of premium performance cars. What was the best way to keep up in the escalating power race between Germany's big three, BMW, Mercedes-Benz, and Audi? More complexity, more cylinders, and ever-higher revs? Or forced induction in the shape of superchargers or turbos?

BMW's eventual choice of the latter saw it fall into line with its competitors. As we saw in the preceding chapter, M Division's first generation of turbocharged cars certainly did tick all the boxes when it came to technical values such as more power, higher performance, and greater efficiency, and even economy. But where those cars missed out was in the area of more subjective perceptions, particularly throttle response, engine noise, and the sense of driver involvement, itself a key core M value. For M engineers, this might be interpreted as a failure, a box not ticked. So, true to Kawamoto's thinking, M GmbH took this unfamiliar sense of customer unease to heart and set about ensuring that the second generation of each of its most important turbo model lines would swing the balance decisively back into the positive.

The major change for the F90-generation M5 was the introduction of all-wheel drive. Several different modes were available to the driver, including the track-only RWD demonstrated here by a BMW test driver.

M5 F90: 600-Horsepower Turbo, Automatic, All-Wheel Drive—and Back in the Groove

True to BMW tradition, when the G30—the seventh generation of the company's staple 5-Series sedan—was first announced late in 2016, it did not differ dramatically from its F10 predecessor, though clever refinements made its aerodynamics significantly better. And under the skin were major improvements, including the extensive use of aluminum to save some 100 kilograms overall, sophisticated chassis systems such as Integral Active Steering for the rear wheels, and a major step-up in electronic content to provide safety features and connectivity at the ready for eventual autonomous operation. Among the engine options at launch were the plug-in hybrid 530e, with 252 horsepower, and the 462-horsepower V-8–powered M550i xDrive, complete with all-wheel drive.

Carrying the M prefix, the M550i was of course developed under the close eye of M GmbH. But to the relief of BMW aficionados worldwide, it was not to be M's last word on the G30 generation: as early as August the same year, BMW announced the impending arrival of a new M5, the sixth to carry that designation. It was advertised as the most advanced version to date, one that would major on efficiency as well as outright performance. Significantly, however—and to the dismay of some hard-core M fans—BMW also announced that the new M5 would feature all-wheel drive and a torque converter automatic gearbox. Both of these developments, the true believers complained, pointed in the direction of a softening of the M5's appeal and the start down a slippery slope toward comfort and convenience as the model's main priorities.

They need not have worried. BMW, again true to the M5's historical mission, had hit upon a sweet spot that allowed the new car to be all things to all people: discreet and luxurious when off-duty, but able to deliver stunning performance and thrilling dynamics when roused. This time, the commentators were united: after the disappointment of the outgoing model, this new one was a return to top form for BMW. One magazine proclaimed it the best M5 since the E39. BMW has upped its game, said another.

The new car was naturally even quicker than its predecessor and the M5 before that. Yet, with the S63 V-8 still rated at 600 horsepower despite revised twin turbos and upgraded management software, it no more than matched the old car in terms of horsepower. Instead, the performance gains—with 100 kilometers per hour now reached in 3.4 seconds—came through lighter weight (even allowing for the AWD system), an eight-speed gearbox, and the general increases in efficiency prompted by a single central control module coordinating a vast range of functions. The intelligent M xDrive all-wheel-drive system was calibrated to retain BMW's familiar rear-wheel-drive feel, with torque only added to the fronts once the rears could no longer cope alone. What's more, and to please the exhibitionist contingent, there was a selectable pure RWD mode intended for track use and accompanied by warnings on the central display screen.

M5 drivers were able to configure the car's dynamic systems to their own personal preferences via the iDrive controller and the clear central display. Here [top] is the menu overseeing chassis systems, while [above] the sub-menu shows that rear-wheel drive has been selected.

One of BMW's strongest selling messages for the M5's AWD system was its added safety—and that it allowed drivers to perform controlled drifts. The consensus was that the new model was more engaging than its predecessor.

All suspension components were stiffened and rethought for extreme M demands, and this even extended to extra crossmembers and ball joints instead of flexible bushings. The steering remained electrohydraulic rather than moving to fully electric, and again the braking system was either M Compound or, at extra cost, M Carbon Ceramic. A redesigned front bumper fed extra cooling airflow to the multiple heat exchangers that took care of the engine, turbos, charge air cooling, transmission, and air conditioning; the large roof panel was lightweight carbon fiber composite, the widened front fenders and hood panel were aluminum, and a discreet rear apron gave space to the four exhaust outlets.

Inside, the driver was confronted with a myriad of settings controlling the engine, transmission, steering, dampers, and Dynamic Stability Control. Learning the lessons of previous generations, these many permutations were simplified through the Drive Performance Control, giving the choice of Efficient, Sport, and Sport Plus modes, with preferred settings storable for recall via the twin M buttons on the steering wheel. The system was further simplified with the M5's facelift three years later, giving quicker direct access to the required settings and iDrive menus. To reassure buyers that the M5 had not gone soft, the seats adopted a clearer racing style (but were still electrically adjusted and heated) and the standard head-up display would switch to M view with F1-type upshift lights when Sport was selected.

◀▲ Markets such as the UK chose to take only the pricier Competition version of the M5, distinguishable by its black grille surrounds.

In early 2021, BMW launched the first-ever CS edition of an M5, a hard-core derivative with weight savings of 70 kilograms and an engine further uprated to 635 horsepower—making it BMW's fastest ever production model. Among the interior changes were a move to four bucket seats, with those in the front being lightweight carbon fiber.

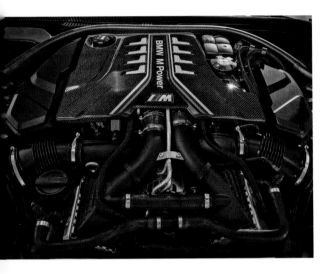

"The new BMW M5 drives like a rear-wheel-powered vehicle, but with more traction," M Division president Frank van Meel assured reporters and customers—and it truly did. The countless thousands of miles spent hammering around the Nürburgring's Nordschleife and other development circuits had clearly paid off: this was manifestly a fabulously capable and enjoyable super-sedan despite its impeccably tailored suit, shirt, and tie.

Few found reason to argue with BMW over its move to all-wheel drive and automatic transmission, for the simple and incontestable reason that this car could do everything that the outgoing car could do. And more, and better. Spectacular sustained tire-smoking drifts? Dragster-style acceleration off-the-line, powering unstoppably to 300 kilometers per hour? A luxurious evening cruise to the opera in sumptuous surroundings? All of these, and most between, too, were comfortably within this M5's repertoire thanks to the expertise of M-Division engineers and their skill in harnessing the electronic systems that enabled this large executive sedan to ride like a limousine one moment and handle like a sports car the next.

"This is a proper BMW M super-saloon, and I am extremely happy that the M Division has found its groove again," wrote Tom Ford in *Top Gear*. "This I like. A lot."

Few subsequent changes were made, apart from the familiar addition of a Competition derivative with the volume turned up to 625 horsepower and, in

summer 2019, a limited-edition M5 35 Jahre special. When it came to the midcareer update in summer 2020, there was little on an engineering level that required revision. The only changes that year were cosmetic touches such as the larger, black-rimmed grille and ergonomic improvements to the iDrive controller to allow direct access to the dynamics menus of the greatest interest to M customers.

Just as this book goes to press in the first quarter of 2021, BMW has announced a further development of the F90 M5. The new CS version is the first-ever hard-core M5: with 635 horsepower, it is the most powerful as well as the fastest BMW ever made, and it makes impressive weight savings of 70 kilograms, too, through lightweighting innovations such as carbon fiber bucket seats.

So will the F90 M5, still in full production at the time of writing, have the right ingredients to qualify as one of the all-time greats? Quite possibly. It is already clear that the 600-plus horsepower bracket is nudging the limits of what might be judged socially acceptable in the climate-conscious twenty-first century, and that the high-revving twin-turbo S63 V-8 might mark something of a high point in the art of combustion engine design. More likely, as M Division responds to tomorrow's challenge of pushing dynamics in an altogether different direction and developing cars that are environmentally impeccable as well as thrilling to drive, this M5 will come to be seen as the ultimate expression of its type, the last truly great, classically powered high-performance luxury sedan. That, for sure, will ensure it a place in auto history.

Small is sensational: BMW's compact hotshot rekindled the magic of early M3s with outrageous power and highly responsive dynamics. The final CS version is regularly cited as one of the best M Cars ever.

Small Is Sensational: M2 F87 Is a Thrilling M Masterpiece

There's always been a touch of the wild child in the high-performance versions of BMW's smallest models. For all its engineering sophistication, the 2002tii of the late 1960s was also a pretty edgy car at the limit, and its direct Turbo descendant, the first product of the nascent Motorsport organization, became notorious for its knife-edged dynamics. Then, in 1985, the very first M3 turned the cultivated E30 sedan into a thrillingly raw and rebellious racer. It was hardly surprising that the hard-liners among the M fan club's founding members soon began to resent the growing refinement and indulgent pampering provided by later M Cars as those models grew in girth, cylinder count, and—horror of horrors—luxury appointments.

Reconnecting with that original and slightly anarchic M spirit was one of the key missions of the E82 1-Series M Coupé back in 2011 (see chapter 9): it was a spur-of-the-moment gap-filling model that polarized opinions not just because of its truncated two-door profile but also because of the lurid dynamics born of its surfeit of power over the grip afforded by its chunky tires.

Recognizing that the short-lived 1M Coupé had, for all its waywardness, struck an emotional chord among M fans, BMW needed a follow-up if it wanted to prevent those customers defecting to rival brands. So, after a three-year hiatus, the M2 emerged in late 2015, bearing a striking similarity to its predecessor for the simple reason that BMW had by then rebadged the 1-Series Coupé and Convertible as 2-Series models, making only token styling and engineering changes.

For the M2 version, however, the changes were more fundamental. Though taking as its basis the M235i derivative, the new model was an authentic M Car in every respect. The short, stubby body, with its minimal overhangs and comically swollen arches, grew more serious in intent thanks to a remodeled front with gaping inlets for cooling air; the inspiration for the multiple openings was said to come from the legendary 3.0 CSL. The now even broader wheelarches were more skillfully integrated into the bodysides and carried cutout slots to aid brake cooling, while a fresh diffuser added a touch of muscular menace to the wider-looking rear.

Yet BMW engineers chose an unusual way to address the old model's twitchiness: they added even more power. Billed as an entirely new engine specifically developed for this car, the M2's twin-turbo S55 B30TO straight six gave no less than 370 horsepower and up to 500 Nm of torque, launching the compact 1,625-kilogram bulldog to 100 kilometers per hour in 4.3 seconds with the optional seven-speed M-DCT transmission fitted. The engine differed from that in the M3 and M4 by virtue of its single twin-scroll turbo, as opposed to the bigger cars' twin single-scroll devices. But in other respects, the M2 followed M4 practice, with lightweight aluminum suspension components, rigid subframe-body attachments, forged wheels, and upgraded brakes. Though the steering was M's first with purely electric assistance, two settings were provided, and the transmission and engine characteristics could also be adjusted by the driver.

As if any more proof for the M2's pugnacious and exhibitionist character were needed, its array of driver-selectable modes even included a Smoky Burnout setting—presumably for impressing onlookers and boosting the business of local tire suppliers. Priced at €53,000 and with scant space for four, however, the M2 quickly attracted enthusiastic reviews from commentators excited by its prodigious performance, its compact packaging, and an involving nature reminiscent of the original M3. Yes, there were still a few rough edges, they said, but it showed BMW had gotten back in touch with its Motorsport roots.

Opposite ends of the M spectrum: the M2 CS and the mighty M8 Gran Coupé were unveiled by M GmbH CEO Markus Flasch at the 2019 Los Angeles show.

The M2 went on to be a big commercial hit, becoming M GmbH's top seller in 2017. But it was to go on to even greater things as it evolved over the next two years, culminating in the final M2 CS version that was universally lauded as the true heir of the M3 tradition and declared by *Autocar* to be "possibly the best car in the world for power-on front-engine-rear-drive dynamics." Indeed, in interviews for this book carried out in summer 2020, prior to the launch of the G80 M3 and M4, several of M Division's top executives declared the M2 CS to be the model that most faithfully represented the ethos of the M brand.

Paving the way to the CS in 2020 was the 2018 Competition model, which followed the familiar M practice of offering more power—in this case an upgrade to 410 horsepower—thanks to twin single-scroll turbos and a higher rev limit. The 100-kilometer-per-hour mark was now reached in 4.2 seconds and, with the optional M Driver's pack, the M2 was now good for an outrageous 275 kilometers per hour.

Underlining the serious nature of this upgrade were the full cooling package of the M4, comprising two side radiators in addition to the main central matrix, oil cooler,

and transmission cooler. Externally, the grille was enlarged and finished in black. Further tweaks to the suspension and an impressive pair of carbon fiber strut braces under the hood served to improve steering precision, said BMW, while the electronic Dynamic Stability Control was completely recalibrated so that, in BMW's words, the traction control would not intervene during drifts. This assertion gave a strong clue to the priorities of the M2's customer base and, reflecting this, the enthusiast magazines described the Competition as even more engaging and playful. Besides, at barely €5,000 more than the standard car, it was a bargain by BMW M standards.

No one was sure whether that same description could be applied to the M2 CS when it was first announced in late 2019, priced at gulp-inducing €89,000—almost double the price of the base model. Just as the M3 CSL three generations before had taken some time to be properly appreciated, the M2's price hike appeared to be quite steep for relatively few additional features and only a modest increase in engine power. Yet, again just as with the CSL, the CS proved to be more than the sum of its parts and—again like the CSL—it hit that elusive but all-important sweet spot of being a car that was brilliant on the racetrack, thrilling but also predictable and trustworthy on the public road, and an easy companion in everyday driving.

What did the trick was a combination of seemingly insignificant changes that gave extra sparkle not just to outright performance but also, most vitally for an M model, to the driver's sense of engagement. The engine, also designated S55 B30TO, was boosted to 444 horsepower and its red line raised to a lofty 7,600 rpm, helping shorten the 0–100 kilometer-per-hour sprint to 4.0 seconds and lift the top speed to 280 kilometers per hour. Carbon fiber components, including the reshaped and air-scooped hood, sandwich roof, race-style front splitter, and rear deck spoiler helped improve the aerodynamics as well as save weight, while matte gold V-spoke forged wheels added a key external identification point.

It all worked magically well, thanks in part to the adoption of Adaptive M suspension with three selectable modes to give the best of all worlds—a halfway-decent ride in everyday conditions, just the right amount of body control for fast driving, and a terrific sense of stability close to the limit on circuit. Carbon brakes made their first appearance on the options list, though the regular six-piston stoppers were easily up to the task of slowing the 1,650-kilogram machine.

The final 444 horsepower M2 CS hit that elusive sweet spot between everyday usability, thrilling road dynamics, and brilliant track performance. Key details helped save weight and forged a strong link with racing versions—the race car even retained the dashboard of the regular CS.

Suddenly the M2 found itself being compared with exotic sports cars rather than hatches and sedans in the magazines, with particular praise for its razor-sharp steering. "This is a sensationally good car to drive on the road, and one that doesn't come apart on the track," reported *Autocar*: "It is finer, sharper, keener—though no lighter than standard—and could just give the top spec Porsche 718 Cayman a good scrap."

"In a time when BMW is changing so much about itself, from the way it makes cars to the way it designs them," added *BMW Blog*, "it's refreshing to drive such a simple BMW; one that reminds us of what the brand is known for. Forget the BMW M8 Competition, with its world-destroying performance. It's the M2 CS you want to properly drive."

The erstwhile bad boy had indeed begun to behave better: the drive on the wild side was no longer quite so outrageously scary, but it was a lot faster, a lot more resourceful—and a whole lot more fun.

The 2021 M4 and M3: the inclusion of all-wheel drive, automatic transmission, and extravagant styling saw this fresh generation grow up in terms of sophistication and presence, but manual transmission and rear-wheel drive were retained as options to please hard-core fans.

2021 M3 and M4 G80-83—the Last of the Great Pedigree Performance Cars?

The fifty-year story of BMW M Division's core models, such a vital emotional touchstone for the brand's international fan base of sports car enthusiasts, comes right up to date with the 2021 M3 sedan and M4 Coupé.

First revealed to the media and online in September 2020 as part of a highly orchestrated launch buildup, the sixth-generation M3 sedan and its M4 Coupé counterpart entered production in the final quarter of the year in Munich and Dingolfing, respectively. The reasons for the protracted buildup were multiple. Perhaps the most sensitive was how the cars were going to look, in particular the prominent twin vertical grilles that dominated the front. This aggressive new style had been previewed in two show cars, the Vision iNext and the Concept i4, and it had not been well received. Some early hints in photos of disguise-wrapped cars out on test helped soften up opinion.

The cars' technical specifications were published early, too, for BMW knew full well that diehard M fans would balk at two key aspects of the M3 and M4's makeup, both of which risked being interpreted as a dilution of its sporting credentials: first, the move to a torque-converter automatic transmission in place of the racy M-DCT double clutch and, second, the provision of all-wheel drive, again something seen as alien in highly focused sports coupés. Though these two features had already proved themselves successful in the larger M5 of 2017, the more purist clientele for the M3 and M4 might not be so happy—BMW must have reasoned it would be a good idea to get the shocks out of the way ahead of the launch. Further prelaunch releases revealed that BMW was working on a Touring version of the M3 too. This, along with the five-door Gran Coupé style previewed in the Concept i4, pointed toward a much-expanded lineup of perhaps five body styles: four-door M3 sedan, five-door M3 Touring station wagon, two-door M4 Coupé, five-door M4 Gran Coupé, and M4 soft-top Convertible.

There were still some surprises when the core M3 and M4 were unveiled in the third quarter of 2020. Predictably, many expressed outrage at the brash new portrait-format grilles and the confrontational frontal design, though others were quick to recall that the fuss over Chris Bangle's E65 7-Series in 2001 had died down within a matter of months. More surprising was the sheer breadth of choice available: the eight-speed automatic was not compulsory, as a six-speed manual was also available; the M xDrive all-wheel-drive setup was optional, too, and instead of coming six months down the line the Competition option was available right from the get-go. These options applied to both the M3 sedan and the M4 Coupé, the only body styles revealed at the launch. All in all, it was clear that BMW had not neglected the diehard pure-M fans.

Built on the company's modular Cluster Architecture (CLAR) platform, the new cars were longer and wider than their predecessors and, true to the M ethos, they were faster and more powerful too. The standard version of the S58 B30TO straight six engine was listed at 480 horsepower at 6,250 rpm, along with peak torque of

◤ The four-door M3 sedan was just as capable of extreme on-track antics as the sleek M4 Coupé. As with the M5, numerous driver-configurable systems could deliver a tailor-made driving experience.

▼ The grille. Enough said.

The 2021 M4 is scarcely recognizable as a descendant of the original M3 of the 1980s, having grown in every dimension and boasting nearly three times the power. But what links all the generations is M's unrivaled dynamic experience.

550 Nm from 2,650 to 6,130; for the Competition model, the figures rose to 510 horsepower and 650 Nm. Driving through the eight-speed Steptronic automatic, the standard models claimed 0–100 kilometer-per-hour acceleration in 4.2 seconds and the Competition editions 3.9 seconds. In all cases, the claimed top speeds were 250 kilometers per hour, or 290 kilometers per hour with the optional M Driver's Package.

While the suspension, braking, cooling, and lubrication systems all received the familiar bespoke M-style upgrades, the new-generation models did introduce several innovative features to further broaden the range of dynamic options available to the driver. For the first time on any midsize M model, the driver was given the choice of two braking modes, Comfort and Sport, and, as part of the M Drive Professional pack, BMW introduced ten-stage adjustability for the traction control system, giving drivers precise regulation of the preferred intervention level for wheelspin mitigation. This system was integrated into the M-Dynamic mode, one of whose settings now allowed controlled drifts. There was even an M Drift Analyzer built into the onboard electronics to record the oversteer and opposite lock episodes on the driver's hot laps and captured by the BMW M Laptimer app on their iPhone.

The profusion of electronic systems led BMW to simplify the driver's task by grouping all the safety assist, navigation, and display functions under the M Mode button on the center console. All the systems relating to the car's dynamic behavior

were regrouped under the central Setup button, giving direct access to no fewer than seven sets of alternative powertrain and chassis parameters, not forgetting the separate settings for the GearShift Assistant on manual cars, the M xDrive settings on AWD models, and the ten Traction Control settings of the Professional pack.

The task faced by potential buyers navigating the BMW Configurator was probably no less daunting. With this G80 generation, the scope and volume of personalization options expanded exponentially. Take brakes, for instance: the choice was not only between M Compound or M Carbon Ceramic rotors, but also three different colors of calipers plus a gold for Carbon; the forged wheels were offered in two styles and four colors. And then the buyer was faced with a further host of carbon add-ons, both interior and exterior, to complement the existing standard carbon roof.

While it might be hard to recognize the genes of the original raw and racy M3 of thirty-five years ago in either of these cars—they have almost three times the horsepower and are half as much again in weight—today's market demands that they serve a vastly broader audience. For M-Division engineers, that places the bar still higher: these cars must be comfortable, refined, and easy to drive in day-to-day conditions, while also delivering the thrilling track-based driving experience demanded by hard-core M fans.

Raw 510-horsepower racer or civilized transcontinental luxury GT? The M4 seeks to be all things to all buyers, and the onward march of electronic controls has been kept in check with key functions still accessible via physical buttons and switches.

Time warp: BMW toyed with the idea of a Touring station wagon version of its E46 M3 in the early 2000s, and now a wagon edition has been confirmed for the latest G80 generation.

"The balance between superior performance and unrestricted everyday suitability so typical of an M attains a new level," said Markus Flasch, chairman of the board of BMW M GmbH. "With each BMW M automobile, we put motorsport technology on the road."

Nowhere is this more important than with the M3 and M4, M Division's most dynamic and emblematic models and the cars that are seen by the enthusiast community as M's brand heroes—the most extreme expressions of BMW's dynamic values. The F90 M5, with its immense array of sophisticated dynamics systems, showed that the seemingly incompatible extremes of luxury and agile supersports performance can indeed be combined in a single vehicle, to keep everyone happy. While this may not be so simple when it comes to the M3 and M4's more diversified clientele, the new cars do offer enthusiasts a lot more choice of engineering layout and, polarizing style aside, all the signs indicate that M Division has once again played its cards with great skill.

ROY
LICHTENSTEIN
1977
BMW 320I

ANDY
WARHOL
1979
BMW M1

ERNST
FUCHS
1982
BMW 635 CSI

ROBERT
RAUSCHENBERG
1986
BMW 635 CSI

MICHAEL JAGAMARA
NELSON
1989
BMW M3

BMW Art Car retrospective Assembled in Munich's BMW Welt are (top picture, left to right) David Hockney's 1995 850 CSi, Jeff Koons' 2010 M3 GT2, A.R. Penck's 1991 Z1, César Manrique's 730i from 1990, and Ernst Fuchs' 635 CSi, painted in 1982. The lower picture shows Roy Lichtenstein's 1977 320i race car, the Andy Warhol M1 from 1979, and Robert Rauschenberg's 635 CSi dating from 1986.

M2 (F87)

Model name and code

M2, F87	M2 CS, F87

Claim to fame

Wild-child compact hotshot rekindled magic of early M3s; power, poise, and thrills, despite some rough edges	Exciting return to M's roots: fast, raw, and highly responsive. One of the very best

Years in production

2014–2020	2019

Number built

60,020 (all models)	n/a

Launch price

€53,000	€89,200

Engine code and type

S55B30TO, straight six, DOHC 24 valve, Valvetronic variable valve timing, twin turbo	S55B30TO, straight six, DOHC 24 valve, Valvetronic variable valve timing, twin turbo

Displacement, cc

2,979	2,979

Peak power hp @ rpm

370@6,500	444@6,250

Max torque, Nm @ rpm

465@1,400–5,650 plus 35 Nm overboost	550@2,350–5,000

Transmission and drive

6-speed manual, rear, Active M differential	7-speed M-DCT dual-clutch automatic, rear, Active M differential

Suspension, front

Double wishbones, control arms, coil-spring/damper units	Double wishbones, control arms, coil-springs, Adaptive M dampers

Suspension, rear

Five-link axle, coil springs	Five-link axle, coil springs, Adaptive M dampers

Body styles

Two-door coupé	Two-door coupé

Curb weight, kg

1,625	1,650

Max speed (km/h) and 1–100 km/h (sec)

250 (restricted)/274; 4.5 (4.3 with M-DCT)	250 (restricted)/280; 4.0

Production by year (all models)

2020	9,428
2019	12,992
2018	14,501
2017	14,961
2016	7,906
2015	226
2014	6
Grand total	60,020

M5 (F90)

Model name and code

M5, F90

Claim to fame

Gen-2 turbo M5 has AWD, auto, and huge power; insanely fast but sharper, safer, more engaging—a brilliant all-rounder

Years in production

2016–present

Number built

22,886 (through 2020)

Launch price

€107,250

Engine code and type

S63B44T4, 90-degree V-8, DOHC per bank, 32-valve twin turbo

Displacement, cc

4,395

Peak power hp @ rpm

600

Max torque, Nm @ rpm

750

Transmission and drive

8-speed M Steptronic automatic, xDrive all-wheel drive, active torque distribution, Active M rear differential

Suspension, front

Double wishbones, coil spring/damper units, lateral control arms

Suspension, rear

Five-link compound axle with control arms, coil springs, electronically controlled dampers

Body styles

Four-door sedan

Curb weight, kg

1,950

Max speed (km/h) and 1–100 km/h (sec)

250 (restricted) or 305 with optional M Driver's Pack; 3.4

Production by year

2020	4,020
2019	6,511
2018	11,726
2017	573
2016	56
Grand total through 2020	22,886

For a key to specification tables, see page 221

M3 & M4 (G80-83)

Model name and code	
M3, G80	M4, G82
Claim to fame	
Second turbo M3 has more power, optional automatic, and AWD, promising wider appeal without losing keen edge	2021 M4 reflects M3 upgrades to cater for higher power and broader customer base; options allow new choice of drivelines
Years in production	
2018–present	2019–present
Launch price	
€91,200 (Competition)	€93,000 (Competition)
Engine code and type	
S58B30T0, straight six, DOHC 24-valve, Valvetronic, twin turbochargers	S58B30T0, straight six, DOHC 24 valve, Valvetronic, twin turbochargers
Displacement, cc	
2,979	2,979
Peak power hp @ rpm	
480@6,250 Competition: 510@6250	480@6,250 Competition: 510@6250
Max torque, Nm @ rpm	
550@2,650–6,130 Competition: 650@2,750–5,500	550@2,650–6,130 Competition: 650@2,750–5,500
Transmission and drive	
6-speed manual, rear-wheel drive or optional M xDrive AWD	6-speed manual, rear-wheel drive or optional M xDrive AWD
Alternative transmission	
8-speed M-Steptronic automatic	8-speed M-Steptronic automatic
Suspension, front	
Double wishbones, control arms, coil-spring/damper units	Double wishbones, control arms, coil-spring/damper units
Suspension, rear	
Five-link axle, coil springs, electronically controlled dampers	Five-link axle, coil springs, electronically controlled dampers
Body styles	
Four-door sedan, five-door Touring wagon	Two-door coupé and convertible
Curb weight, kg	
1,705 1,730 (Competition)	1,700 (Coupé) 1,725 (Competition)
Max speed (km/h) and 1–100 km/h (sec)	
250 (restricted)/290; 4.2 (Competition: 3.9)	250 (restricted)/290; 4.2 (Competition: 3.9)

Production by year

2020	428	2020	211
2019	94	2019	31
2018	5	Grand total through 2020	242
Grand total through 2020	527		

M6, M8

THE HIGH-END COUPÉS

Lavish lifestyle meets racetrack dynamics: a recipe for success?

11

Launched in 2018, the M8 saw BMW's big coupé/cabriolet duo upgraded to the true luxury segment, becoming the brand's technology flagship and its global ambassador for style and glamour.

The third generation M6 Coupé had the grace and harmony that were lacking in its predecessor, but its M5-derived chassis and V-8 turbo marked the end of the high-revving V-10 engine. Post-facelift Competition models boosted power to 600 horsepower, but the weight penalty of its sumptuous specification meant the 2011 M6 was more of a grand tourer than a raw sports car.

THE ORIGINAL 1986 E30 M3 and the 1985 E28-generation M5 sedan are rightly seen as central to the mythology of M-Division cars, but even the most ardent fans tend to forget that the very first series-produced road car to wear the M badge was an elegant, high-end coupé. Yet in contrast to the unbroken run of M3s and M5s in BMW's M catalog, those big coupés have only appeared from time to time—and some would even contend that the models that came after the 1984 original have struggled to match that model's ecstatic reception.

The original 6-Series dated back to 1976 and was based on engineering elements of 5-Series sedan models current at the time. The 6 was not an instant hit, and it took the hot twenty-four-valve engine from the M1 supercar to put the coupé on the performance map in 1984. That was the M635CSi or, for the North American market, the first M6. The 6-Series coupé's timeless elegance and the compelling dynamics of the M6 version kept it in production through until the end of the 1980s. Sadly, it had no direct successor, as the mighty V-12–powered 8-Series coupé had been waiting in the wings for some time. BMW Motorsport did develop an M version of the big 8, but it never made production.

M customers had to wait a full sixteen years for the 6-Series nameplate to be revived. It came in the controversial Chris Bangle–styled form of the 2003 E63 645 CSi Coupé and Convertible, with M6 versions (see chapter 7) appearing in 2005, complete with the screaming V-10 engine, the unloved SMG III transmission, and the chassis systems of the E60 M5 sedan. When this M6 finally went out of production in September 2010, with 14,152 Coupés and Convertibles built, it marked the end of an era as the extravagant V-10 disappeared at the same time. A rather shorter hiatus followed the E63's demise, its replacement again based on the recently released M5 sedan: the 2012 F10 model that had made the daring switch from ten cylinders to a twin-turbo V-8.

Like its predecessor and the M8 that succeeded the M6 in 2019, the mission of the mid-2010s big coupés was to tread a notoriously tricky tightrope: would they aim to be an out-and-out sports car to compete with the likes of the Porsche 911, or would they adopt the allure of a more luxurious—but nevertheless very fast—GT car, capable of crossing continents in comfort and style? Given M Division's celebrated skills in turning regular BMW sedans into track-capable hotshots, it is perhaps disappointing that these super-coupés and convertibles have not earned themselves a higher profile within the M repertoire. They have a definite following, for sure, but appreciation for these cars is not as strong or as unshakeable as that enjoyed by their less glamorously styled brothers.

Pure Sports or Luxury GT? Identity Crisis for the M6, F06—F12/13

There was a clear sense of relief as BMW unveiled the new 6-Series in early 2011: the long, flowing lines of both the Coupé and the Convertible versions brought an air of grace and harmony that had been lacking in the outgoing model, which had disappeared from the BMW catalog the year before. Before long, a third model had been added—the stylish Gran Coupé, with a longer wheelbase and the low, rakish coupé profile stretched in the rear compartment to provide a set of rear doors and a surprising amount of space in the back.

The M versions arrived over the next two years, all three of them based as usual on the platform and engineering content of the current F10 M5 sedan. This meant the formidable S63 twin-turbo V-8 engine, delivering the compelling peak power figure of 560 horsepower between 6,000 and 7,000 rpm and feeding it to the rear wheels via the M5's seven-speed M-DCT transmission. BMW bragged at the time of the "intense M experience" promised by the new M6 models, noting that they were not only faster and more powerful than their forebears, but 30 percent more efficient too.

Carbon ceramic brakes were the principal listed option, though North American customers where offered an alternative six-speed manual gearbox if desired. Only a handful took up the option.

BMW's pricing policy saw the M6 nudge ever closer to the six-figure mark in Sterling terms, and though there was praise for the new car's style and specifications, concerns were voiced over the 30 percent price premium compared with the equivalent M5—especially as the latter had much more space, equipment, and comfort. Both cars did, however, attract negative comments when it came to ride quality, even in the most forgiving of the three chassis settings. On performance there could be no discussion, with 100 kilometers per hour dispatched in 4.2 seconds and a top speed of over 300 kilometers per hour available to buyers prepared to pay the extra for the M Driver's Pack.

The Competition Pack models that followed in the M6's second year brought an extra 15 horsepower thanks to revised boost mapping, along with upgrades to the suspension, quicker steering, 20-inch wheels, and new software for the Active M differential. With a light facelift introduced in mid-2015, the grille was enlarged and, on Competition versions, power was raised to a solid 600 horsepower; the suspension was further enhanced with fresh springs, dampers, and anti-roll bars. *Autocar* was equivocal about this version, complaining that there was "some lag" in the engine response "before an inordinate amount of shove arrives," noting that the M6 needed a derestricted *Autobahn* to get the best out of it.

Traveling in style: for many customers, the M6 made more sense as a spectacularly fast four-seater Convertible, with its more supple suspension; the stylish low-riding four-door Gran Coupé was introduced later and became a niche success in the elite business segment.

Of the three body styles, the four-door Gran Coupé was perhaps the best received in the market, selling well against direct competitors such as the Audi RS7 and the AMG versions of Mercedes-Benz's CLS class, not to mention the Porsche Panamera. The muscular but not too intensely hardline character of the M treatment appeared better suited to the Gran Coupé's classy four-seater format than to that of the regular Coupé, where many had perhaps hoped it might have been a more closely focused rival for the Porsche 911.

M8 F91-93: BMW's Flagship Majors on Power and Technology

As befits a model series beginning with the figure eight, the replacement for the 6-Series announced in 2018 was positioned right from the start above the 7-Series as BMW's flagship model—its global ambassador for style and glamour. Naturally it majored on technical innovation, too, and, in the case of the M8 versions that began to reach customers in 2019, extreme performance.

The story began in spring 2017 at the exclusive Concorso d'Eleganza at the Villa d'Este in the Italian Lakes. BMW chose this prestigious event to unveil its Concept 8, a sleek two-door luxury coupé finished in dark blue, featuring a distinctly Aston Martin allure in its profile, especially the rear of the glasshouse. To no one's surprise, the company announced the development of an 8-Series and said it was working flat-out on an M model too. BMW also revealed that it was working on a parallel M8 GTE racing version that would bring the company back to the 24 Hours of Le Mans the following year.

The 8-Series launch program got into full swing at the March 2018 Geneva motor show with the four-door Concept M8 Gran Coupé, clearly more production ready and sending an obvious challenge to the likes of Porsche and Mercedes. The production Coupé premiered at Le Mans the same summer. When manufacture began at Dingolfing in late summer, the top model listed was the M850i xDrive, with a 530-horsepower V-8, Steptronic automatic transmission, and all-wheel drive courtesy of BMW's intelligent xDrive system.

Keen to show the world that the new M8 was a proper sports car and not just a luxury coupé, BMW began a racing program with M8 GTEs even before the road car had launched. For a heavyweight coupé, the roadgoing M8 Competition was remarkably good on track.

As the technology flagship for the whole BMW group, the M8 represented the last word in luxurious, high-tech fittings and equipment, and boasted the company's most powerful engine ever. Innovations included driver-selectable brake response settings, but by now the model's price had climbed past Porsche and into Aston Martin and Bentley territory.

Among the engineering highlights were Integral Active steering, which swiveled the rear wheels slightly to improve high-speed stability and low-speed agility. At launch the M8 was priced at a whisker under €120,000, positioning it as a prestigious luxury GT rather than an aspiring sports car. The M8 models arrived in showrooms a short while later amid a flurry of extravagant PR messaging, most notably the boast that the engine was a *Meisterstück*, or masterpiece, and that in the Competition version of the car the V-8 was the most powerful unit BMW had ever built, at 625 horsepower.

In the rest of its engineering the M8 closely followed its M5 mentor, with the eight-speed Steptronic automatic transmission and M xDrive all-wheel drive apportioning drive to all four corners, but with a sporty rearward bias and, as in the M5, the facility to go into RWD mode for track use. Compared with the standard 8-Series, the M versions specified stiffer suspension and extra braces and tie-bars; in addition, Competition editions had much more rigid engine mounts for quicker throttle response.

BMW poured all its technical know-how into the car, giving it adjustable brake-by-wire with a carbon ceramic option, laser lights (again optional), and networking the gearbox with the navigation system so the car would downshift on the approach to a bend and hold on to a lower gear during a sequence of bends. This and the host of other chassis dynamic systems could be controlled through a central Setup button and memorized on the twin red M buttons on the steering wheel. Omitted, however, was the rear-wheel steering of the regular model. The equipment list resembled that of a luxury limousine rather than a sports car, and there was an inevitable penalty on the weighbridge, with a total mass perilously close to two tons. Even so, BMW still claimed "near-supercar levels of performance"—and, strictly speaking, this was true.

The carbon-roofed Coupé hit 60 miles per hour in 3.2 seconds, the fabric-topped Convertible in 3.3, and each would bust the 300 kilometer-per-hour barrier if the optional M Driver's Pack was specified.

In keeping with its role as the flagship for everything BMW stands for, the M8 was priced dramatically higher than its predecessor, with just a few options taking it well past the €160,000 barrier. This represented a dramatic raising of BMW's sights, elevating the 8-Series' targets from the premium to the true luxury segment and bringing it into the orbit of classical superluxury players such as Aston Martin and Bentley.

Early reviewers were far from convinced this was a sensible move. A common thread was that the M8 was exceptionally competent and capable, even on the racetrack, but that it was hard to hide its weight. A good long-distance machine with a cultured, pliable ride, one that devours terrain, said one commentator, while another praised its precise steering and predictable responses when pushed hard; a third welcomed the more relaxed nature of the Convertible with its specific chassis tuning. But all agreed that two things were missing: a sense of engagement and that "M-Car fizz" on one hand and, perhaps harder to pin down, the sheer sense of occasion that comes with an aristocratic marque like Bentley.

"A really grand grand tourer," read one verdict, while another summed it up as "much more 7-Series than true high-octane sports car." Once again, the pundits may have been asking for the impossible, but BMW customers had the last word: more than forty-one thousand 8-Series, nearly one-fifth of them M8 models, found customers in the first three years the model was on the market.

▼ The four-door Gran Coupé version of the M8 offered greater practicality for business use but could not quite match the clean lowrider style of its M6 predecessor.

▼▼ The business end: with an unprecedented 625 horsepower from its turbo V-8 fed through M xDrive all-wheel drive and the Active M differential, the M8 Competition accelerated to 100 km/h in 3.2 seconds and reached a top speed of 305 km/h.

M6 (F06, F12-13)

Model name and code	
M6 Coupé, F13, M8 Convertible, F12	M6 Gran Coupé, F06

Claim to fame	
Essentially an M5 with more glamour: classy and potent, but not sure if it's pure sports or GT	Low-rider with coupé style but four doors and rear seats; a quiet success

Years in production	
2011–2018	2013–2018

Number built	
15,552 (all M6 models)	n/a

Launch price	
€113,000	€117,500

Engine code and type	
S63 B44TO, 90-degree V-8, 32-valve, twin OHC per bank, Valvetronic, twin turbo	S63 B44TO, 90-degree V-8, 32-valve, twin OHC per bank, Valvetronic, twin turbo

Displacement, cc	
4,395	4,395

Peak power hp @ rpm	
560@6,000–7,000	560@6,000–7,000

Max torque, Nm @ rpm	
680@1,500–5,750	680@1,500–5,750

Transmission and drive	
Seven-speed M-DCT dual-clutch automatic, rear axle with Active M differential	Seven-speed M-DCT dual-clutch automatic, rear axle with Active M differential

Alternative transmission	
Six-speed manual (North America only)	Six-speed manual (North America only)

Suspension, front	
Double wishbones with lateral links, coil spring damper units and electronic dampers	Double wishbones with lateral links, coil spring damper units and electronic dampers

Suspension, rear	
Integral multilink with coil springs and electronic dampers	Integral multilink with coil springs and electronic dampers

Body styles	
Two-door coupé and convertible	Four-door coupé

Curb weight, kg	
1,850 (Coupé)	1,875

Max speed (km/h) and 1–100 km/h (sec)	
250 (restricted)/300; 4.2 (Coupé)	250 (restricted)/300; 4.2

Production by year (all models)

2018	308
2017	922
2016	1,500
2015	2,342
2014	2,715
2013	4,736
2012	2,954
2011	75
Grand total	15,552

For a key to specification tables, see page 221

M8 (F91-93)

Model name and code	
M8, F91-92	M8 Gran Coupé, F93
Claim to fame	
Technology-laden luxury taken to the max with huge power and clever chassis, but doesn't crack it as a pure sports car	Extravagant high-tech flagship arguably works better as svelte four-door than rival for 911
Years in production	
2017–present	2019–present
Number built	
7,254 (all versions) through 2020	n/a
Launch price	
€169,700 (Competition)	n/a
Engine code and type	
S63 B44T4, 90-degree V-8, 32-valve, twin OHC per bank, Valvetronic, twin turbo	S63 B44T4, 90-degree V-8, 32-valve, twin OHC per bank, Valvetronic, twin turbo
Displacement, cc	
4,395	4,395
Peak power hp @ rpm	
600@6,000 Competition: 625@6,000	600@6,000 Competition: 625@6,000
Max torque, Nm @ rpm	
750@1,800–5,600	750@1,800–5,600
Transmission and drive	
Eight-speed M Steptronic automatic, M xDrive all-wheel drive with Active M rear differential	Eight-speed M Steptronic automatic, M xDrive all-wheel drive with Active M rear differential
Suspension, front	
Double wishbones, coil springs, lateral control arms, Adaptive M dampers	Double wishbones, coil springs, lateral control arms, Adaptive M dampers
Suspension, rear	
Five-link compound axle with control arms, coil springs and Adaptive M dampers	Five-link compound axle with control arms, coil springs and Adaptive M dampers
Body styles	
Two-door coupé and convertible	Four-door coupé
Curb weight, kg	
1,965 (Coupé)	2,090
Max speed (km/h) and 1–100 km/h (sec)	
250 (restricted)/305; 3.3 (Coupé), 3.2 (Competition)	250; 3.2 (Competition)

Production by year (all M8, through 2020)

2020	3,104
2019	3,986
2018	161
2017	3
Grand total	7,254

A RACE
FOR POWER

The need for speed pushes M's
heavyweight 4x4s into the 600-hp club

12

The success of the big X5M
and X6M led BMW to try
extending the strategy to
the medium sector with
the high-powered X4M
and X3M, pictured right.

BMW COULD BE SAID TO HAVE invented the modern and now hugely profitable SUV segment with its first-generation X5 in 1999. The model was a big hit because it handled as neatly as a passenger car, it was easy to drive, and it steered and braked with confidence rather than protest. Other manufacturers took note and cashed in, but by the time the bigger second-generation X5 came in 2006, BMW was again ahead of the game, supplementing it with a fastback X6 derivative aimed at a sportier, more image-conscious clientele. Both soon spawned high-performance M versions (see chapter 8), to the horror of some commentators but also to the delight of BMW's accountants and buyers seeking to reconcile once-impossible combinations of macho swagger and straightline speed.

Thanks in no small measure to the efforts of M-Division engineers, the boundaries of power, speed, and performance have been pushed far beyond what anyone in 1999 could ever have imagined. The original X5 boasted 286 horsepower and could hit 100 kilometers per hour in a then-impressive 7.0 seconds. Today's X5M, by contrast, has a mighty 625 horsepower, storms to 100 kilometers per hour in 3.8 seconds, and tops out at 290. By anyone's standards that is significant progress, and it appears to be just what a specific subset of attention-seeking customers want.

X5M and X6M, F85/86: The Power War Steps Up a Gear

The first generation of M-developed SUVs had done much more than simply bring in the customers and, with them, a fat slice of BMW's annual profits. On a technical level these models had managed to square what had until then been regarded as an impossible circle: to make a tall and heavy multipurpose off-road vehicle accelerate, brake, steer, and handle like a sports car—or at least like a decent high-performance business sedan.

The menacing coupé-like look of the fresh X6M drew particular criticism when the F85/86 generation launched in 2014. Along with the mechanically similar X5M, they had taken a major step up in stature, power, and weight: now with a much more high-tech chassis, they delivered huge performance despite their weight and bulk.

So for the second generation of the X5M and its X6M companion, BMW decided that the best recipe would be the simplest one: the same, but more of it. The F85/86 M models were unveiled at the 2014 Los Angeles show and went into production in the final quarter of that year. As before, final assembly took place at Spartanburg, South Carolina, using complete drivetrains shipped in from Germany.

That drivetrain was broadly similar, too, with one of the most important differences being the move from six to eight speeds for the automatic transmission. The 4.4-liter S63B44T2 V-8 gained double twin-scroll turbochargers, still housed within the "hot-vee" between the cylinder banks, and rose 4 percent in power to 575 horsepower, bringing the 0–100 kilometer-per-hour acceleration time down to 4.2 seconds. In line with BMW M's "fit for the Nordschleife" policy, all cars with an M in their name had to undergo development on the Nürburgring as well as other test locations: for the M5 and M6 this meant special oil supply arrangements within the engine able to cope with sustained 1.2 g cornering loads, as well as enhanced cooling packs with multiple radiators, heat exchangers, and oil coolers.

Major suspension upgrades implemented by M GmbH engineers included new front wishbone geometry to increase camber and camber progression, a 10mm reduction in ride height, revised bushings and mountings throughout, and the provision of

The biggest differences between the X5M and X6M were to be found at the rear, where many felt the latter's cut-down coupé silhouette to be intimidating. Active Roll Stabilization helped provide surprising agility on and off track for such tall vehicles.

the Active Roll Stabilization system and self-levelling struts at the rear. As with other BMW models, the driver had the choice of several different settings for the principal systems governing dynamics, and the Dynamic Stability Control's M-Dynamic mode even allowed for what BMW described as "mild drifting."

Compared with the previous model, the F85 X5M was more aggressive in its appearance in terms of air intakes, wheelarches, and exhausts, but the F86 X6M went an additional step: its inward-sloping side glass, low roofline, and fastback rear gave it a more powerful hunched stance, emphasized by the kicked-up crease over the rear wheelarches and the complex rear apron with quad exhausts, central diffuser, and inset vents and lights. Mechanically, the pair were identical and drove in a similarly spectacular fashion: clearly very heavy, but with dramatic acceleration when required, and a surprising precision on the road, especially on open roads. Where the mass and bulk were felt most was in quick changes of direction on tighter terrain.

By 2018, when these second-generation M-SUVs were up for replacement, they had attracted a vast army of imitators—from expected quarters such as Audi, Porsche, and Mercedes-Benz, of course, but also from Cadillac, Alfa Romeo, Lexus, Jaguar, and Bentley. Even Lamborghini, Rolls-Royce, and Aston Martin pitched in with their super-premium offerings.

X3M and X4M, F97/98: Mighty Middleweights Miss the Mark

The M-developed versions of BMW's closely related midsize SUV couple were launched in 2019, but their origins go back further—in fact, to the debut of the first-generation X4, itself a direct spinoff of the second iteration of the X3, dating from 2010. The larger X6 is also involved, as its success in the market—despite the squeals of protest from the design community—emboldened BMW to try the same cutdown coupé trick with the smaller X3.

Looking deceptively similar to the luxury-sector X5M and X6M, the midsize X3M and X4M use the same twin-turbo straight six as the high-performance M3.

Enter the downsized X6 as the 2014 X4. Its oddball proportions and detailing again attracted the ire of the taste police. In keeping with its allotted role as the sportier companion to the more practical, more square-rigged X3, the fastback X4 was soon given M treatment—of a sort. The 2015 X4 M40i hosted the world premiere of a new BMW TwinPower turbo straight six engine, giving a generous 355 horsepower and mounted in a chassis that, said BMW, had been specially tuned to M-Performance specifications. Though BMW stopped short of claiming the whole US-built vehicle had been developed by M GmbH engineers, the car won praise for its performance, if not its low-speed ride comfort. That being said, in many ways it set the standard for the inevitable arrival of "authentic" M versions in 2019.

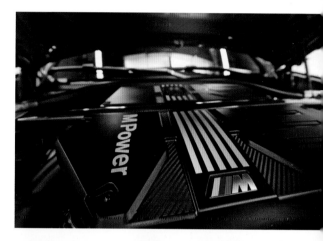

Much anticipation surrounded the release of these models in the spring of 2019. Not only was this the first time these compact SUVs received the attention of BMW's famed M-Division engineers, but the launch was also seen as a dry run for an even more hotly anticipated debut the following year—that of the next-generation M4 and M3, mainstays of the whole M brand. For BMW had let it be known that it was working on an all-new high-performance straight six, and the X3M and X4M were to be its first recipients.

The engine's billing was not exactly modest. "This is the most powerful straight six petrol engine ever to see action in a BMW M Car," ran the press invitation, adding that "it has stunning performance attributes." Indeed, these were no exaggerations: the 3-liter unit, using 3D printing in its construction to achieve internal shapes that would otherwise be impossible to cast, was rated at a heady 480 horsepower in standard form, or an even more remarkable 510 horsepower as a Competition edition. Quoted torque was an impressive 600 Nm in each case, and the rev limit was set at 7,300 rpm, some thousand revs above the peak power point. BMW factory figures gave the Competition version a 0–100 kilometer-per-hour time of just 4.1 seconds, allied to a top speed of 280 kilometers per hour with the M Driver's Pack specified. Twin particulate filters and quadruple catalysts ensured a clean exhaust, apart from CO_2, which nevertheless remained reasonable for the performance at 239 g per kilometer.

The brand-new S58 B30TO straight six had its first application in the X3M and X4M prior to installation in the new M3 and M4. With 480 horsepower in standard form and 510 horsepower in Competition models, it propels the SUVs to 100 km/h in 4.1 seconds.

The new engine was hooked up to the eight-speed Steptronic automatic transmission, M xDrive all-wheel drive, and Active M differential, all familiar from the M5. In terms of their many multiadjustable dynamic systems, the new models were a straightforward copy-and-paste of the M5. With just one exception: there was no facility for a pure 2WD mode, though the DSC did still allow a degree of controlled wheel slip in M-Dynamic mode.

Externally, the cars became more muscular, with 20- or 21-inch wheels, a gloss-black BMW grille on Competition editions, and much larger air inlets at the front to satisfy the engine's thirst for cooling air under intensive use.

Beginning at around €87,000, the price list caused the long-familiar gasp of disbelief accompanying each new M model—but that was nothing in comparison to the verdicts delivered by the first wave of journalists to test the cars. Here was an out-of-character case of BMW M GmbH delivering a new model that turned out to *less* than the sum of its parts: normally, quite the reverse tends to be the rule with M products.

Though equally powerful in its drivetrain to the X4M, the X3M presents a much less confrontational appearance front and rear; the rakish X4M (red) has a more assertive stance and bolder detailing. The driver environments are identical, and both share an enthusiasm for extensive M branding.

Three- and even two-star ratings were the norm as the press corps delighted in the response and power of the new six but bemoaned its synthetic sound and lack of audio bombast. The snappy, highly strung handling that was good on the track fell apart on regular public roads, but the biggest and most universally echoed complaint was the ride comfort—or total lack of it, even with the suspension in its Comfort setting.

"Too firm, too mute, too soulless," wrote *Top Gear*. "It's too much of what we *don't* like about modern cars, and too little of what we love about great BMWs."

That double-edged reprimand from an influential publication is perhaps to be expected, especially given the fact that BMW had urged journalists to regard the X3M and X4M not as hefty SUVs but as sporty sedans that just happened to have a higher build. But below the surface in reporters' critiques of one of BMW's rare missteps lurked a deeper concern: if the new X3M and X4M were serving as a blueprint for the upcoming M3 and M4, was M GmbH losing its touch—and would those near-sacred nameplates turn out to be disappointing two-star cars too?

X5M and X6M, F95/96: Excess All Areas as Greyhound Meets Bus

A wider but slightly less top-heavy look greeted the 2020 model year X5M and X6M, accentuated by the broader and more finely chiseled headlights, larger (and generally black-finished) BMW grilles, and the near-full-width taillight assemblies. The contouring of the bodysides was calmer and more restrained and, though both M models featured purpose-designed front aprons with multiple large air inlet apertures, the overall effect was less aggressive and less confrontational.

Not so the mechanical specifications. Describing the models as "following the classical M blueprint for dynamics, agility, and precision, combined with versatility, extroversion, and modern luxury," BMW upgraded the engine to the latest 600-horsepower specification (or 625 horsepower on Competition versions), stiffening the body structure, installing ultra-high-rigidity engine mountings, and further refining the Adaptive M suspension, steering, and braking systems. Wheels became even bigger, with 21-inch rims at the front and wider, 22-inch ones at the rear.

The communications and control systems were also upgraded to reflect the latest technologies used in other top BMW models. New features included the head-up display, configurable to show standard or sport-level information, or a purely track-focused display, which eliminated all potential distractions such as text messages and navigation prompts.

BMW turned up the power and the bullish presence still further with the F95/96 X5M and X6M generation for the 2020 model year.

One distinctly bling feature that met with some negative press comment was the illuminated grille. To the chagrin of many, this helped start a broader trend within the industry for picking out body features with colored light. In keeping with the "excess all areas" approach of these models, their performance was predictably massive too. Under the headline "Greyhound Meets Bus," *Car*'s Georg Kacher questioned the value of what he described as an X5 with an M5 powertrain, at the same time reeling at its "dynamic talents that make the mind boggle."

Reviewing the new X6M, *Autocar*'s Greg Kable was also ambivalent: "If you're looking for finesse, you best look elsewhere in the M lineup," he wrote. "Although the X6 M is engaging, its driving appeal is not exactly centered on its delicacy of control. Rather, it is the brutish nature of its power delivery and the ability of its gearbox and four-wheel drive system to place its reserves to the road in any one of its various driving modes that make it so memorable."

Extreme sports: tweaks to the twin-turbo V-8 gave up to 625 horsepower on Competition versions for sub-4.0 seconds acceleration to 100 km/h. While the models' sledgehammer performance was beyond doubt, some began to question their increasingly macho image and 290 km/h top speed.

By way of a postscript, the physics-defying sledgehammer performance of this hyper-powered genre of machinery served to spark off an intense debate: should such 600-plus-horsepower blockbusters be allowed to continue or escalate still further? Or should social and political attitudes to climate change and conspicuous consumption determine their future? Companies like Tesla, Jaguar, and Porsche have already shown that spectacular performance can be achieved with zero tailpipe emissions thanks to advanced batteries and electric drive systems. Supercar producers are taking note, too, as are volume manufacturers with their moves to eliminate gasoline and diesel by the mid-2030s.

So will these power SUVs be the last guard to hold out against the electric revolution? And will these muscular bully boys come to be seen as the finest of their breed, or dinosaurs on the verge of extinction?

◀◀ The details that count: customers in the luxury performance SUV sector value design features and clear M branding as much as power and speed. Interiors follow identical themes but the contrasting rear light graphics show how BMW is differentiating the more extrovert X6M from the more practical but equally potent X5M.

X5M & X6M (F85-86)

Model name and code	
X5M, F85	X6M, F86

Claim to fame	
Heavyweight SUV transformed by M into potent and surprisingly responsive 4x4	Steroidal near-supercar performance: aggressive bully boy exterior matches potent, high-tech chassis

Years in production	
2013–2018	2013–2019

Number built	
12,915	9,794

Launch price	
€108,650	€112,150

Engine code and type	
S63 B44T2, 90-degree V-8, 32-valve, twin OHC per bank, Valvetronic, twin turbo	S63 B44T2, 90-degree V-8, 32-valve, twin OHC per bank, Valvetronic, twin turbo

Displacement, cc	
4,395	4,395

Peak power hp @ rpm	
575@6,000–6,500	575@6,000–6,500

Max torque, Nm @ rpm	
750@2,200–5,000	750@2,200–5,000

Transmission and drive	
Eight-speed M Steptronic automatic, xDrive AWD	Eight-speed M Steptronic automatic, xDrive AWD

Suspension, front	
Double wishbones, coil springs, active roll stabilization	Double wishbones, coil springs, active roll stabilization

Suspension, rear	
Multilink axle, self-leveling air springs, active roll stabilization	Multilink axle, self-leveling air springs, active roll stabilization

Body styles	
Five-door SUV	Five-door sports activity coupé

Curb weight, kg	
2,305	2,305

Max speed (km/h) and 1–100 km/h (sec)	
155; 4.2	155; 4.2

Production by year

Year	Built	Year	Built
2018	1,926	2019	438
2017	3,425	2018	1,297
2016	3,125	2017	2,095
2015	4,283	2016	2,259
2014	113	2015	3,581
2013	43	2014	115
Grand total	12,915	2013	9
		Grand total	9,794

X3M & X4M (F97-98)

Model name and code
X3M, F97

Claim to fame
M3/M4 mechanicals transplanted into SUV; great power and speed, but harsh ride and skittish handling

Years in production
2017–present

Number built
10,677 through 2020

Launch price
€87,500

Engine code and type
S58B30TO, straight six DOHC 24-valve, Valvetronic, twin turbo

Displacement, cc
2,993

Peak power hp @ rpm
480@6,250 Competition: 510

Max torque, Nm @ rpm
600@2,600–5,600

Transmission and drive
Eight-speed M Steptronic automatic, M xDrive AWD, Active M rear differential

Suspension, front
Double wishbones, coil springs, Adaptive M dampers

Suspension, rear
Five-link axle with coil springs and Adaptive M dampers

Body styles
Five-door SUV

Curb weight, kg
1,970

Max speed (km/h) and 1–100 km/h (sec)
250 (restricted)/285; 4.2 (Competition: 4.1)

Production by year

Year	Built
2020	2,790
2019	7,759
2018	93
2017	35
Grand total through 2020	10,677

For a key to specification tables, see page 221

X5M & X6M (F95-96)

	X4M, F98	X5M, F95	X6M, F96
Model name and code	X4M, F98	X5M, F95	X6M, F96
Claim to fame	Confrontational looks to match potent engine and taut, twitchy chassis; X3M is less expensive, less flawed	Tall two-ton giant turned into a jumbo jet: sledgehammer power, questionable utility	Style-fixated coupé brother given intense workout: performance beyond doubt but macho image contentious
Years in production	2017–present	2017–present	2018–present
Number built	6,303 through 2020	4,806 through 2020	3,475 through 2020
Launch price	€89,700	€144,300	€144,300
Engine code and type	S58B30TO, straight six DOHC 24-valve, Valvetronic, twin turbo	S63B44T4, 90-degree V-8, DOHC per bank, 32-valve, Valvetronic variable valve timing, twin turbo	S63B44T4, 90-degree V-8, DOHC per bank, 32-valve, Valvetronic variable valve timing, twin turbo
Displacement, cc	2,993	4,395	4,395
Peak power hp @ rpm	480@6,250 Competition: 510	600@6,000 Competition: 625	600@6,000 Competition: 625
Max torque, Nm @ rpm	600@2,600–5,600	750@1,800–5,800	750@1,800–5,800
Transmission and drive	Eight-speed M Steptronic automatic, M xDrive AWD, Active M rear differential	Eight-speed M Steptronic automatic, M xDrive AWD	Eight-speed M Steptronic automatic, M xDrive AWD
Suspension, front	Double wishbones, coil springs, Adaptive M dampers	Double wishbones, coil springs, Adaptive M dampers, active roll stabilization	Double wishbones, coil springs, Adaptive M dampers, active roll stabilization
Suspension, rear	Five-link axle with coil springs and Adaptive M dampers	Multilink axle, self-leveling air springs, Adaptive M dampers, active roll stabilization	Multilink axle, self-leveling air springs, Adaptive M dampers, active roll stabilization
Body styles	Five-door sports activity coupé	Five-door SUV	Five-door sports activity coupé
Curb weight, kg	1,970	2,310	2,295
Max speed (km/h) and 1–100 km/h (sec)	250 (restricted)/280; 4.2 (Competition: 4.1)	250 (restricted)/290; 3.9 (Competition: 3.8)	250 (restricted)/290; 3.9 (Competition: 3.8)

Production by year

X4M, F98		X5M, F95		X6M, F96	
2020	1,694	2020	4,577	2020	3,304
2019	4,523	2019	163	2019	137
2018	79	2018	59	2018	34
2017	7	2017	7	Grand total through 2020	3,475
Grand total through 2020	6,303	Grand total through 2020	4,806		

TURNING DOWN THE HEAT: THE

NEARLY-M
CARS

M-Performance models are a tempting
halfway point to full-house M Cars

13

The BMW i8 sits among
countless other two-
and four-wheeled
treasures in the
company's collection
of classic vehicles such
as the 3.0 CSL, the
BMW-engined Formula
1 championship-
winning Brabham,
and the 1960s Neue
Klasse sedans in the
background.

▲▲ Choice of power: the 5-Series M550i carries an M label and is a halfway house to the full-fledged M5, while the 530e uses plug-in hybrid technology to combine performance with ultralow fuel consumption.

▲ With their engines frequently rivaling gasoline units for power as well as torque, diesel models also come under the M banner. This is the mighty X7 M50d fielding a quad-turbo straight six giving 400 horsepower and 760 Nm torque.

NOT EVERY BMW PRODUCT WITH AN M in its name is a full-fledged, no-expense-spared product of the M GmbH nerve center at Garching, near the main Munich plant in Bavaria. To be sure, the core image-defining M models such as today's M2, M4, M5, and M8 are the ones that must—and invariably do—embody the full extent of M Division's unmatched racetrack-to-road expertise. As such, they reflect the very latest thinking in state-of-the-art engineering, closely focused on outright performance and peak driver involvement. But beneath these leading performers is a much broader cast of supporting actors addressing a more general audience with less specialized requirements and less cash at their disposal.

These second-tier M models, known internally as M-Performance cars, still figure prominently in the M-Division catalog and are just a small step away from that core of "pure" M Cars. Their focus is less exclusively on the driver, and they may incorporate engineering inputs from other disciplines in addition to those supplied by M, but all will have been put through enhanced development programs taking in extensive evaluation on circuits like the Nürburgring Nordschleife and BMW's own Miramas circuit in France. They too are generally regarded as authentic M models and are included in the production totals that M Division posts each year. In 2020, for instance, output of pure M Cars totaled just under thirty-two thousand units, while the M-Performance models accounted for almost three times as many.

These models, such as the M135i, M550i, and Z4 M40i, sit one rung down from the pure M lineup in today's hierarchy. Here the M indicates a version that is more powerful or more sporting than standard, but which has had a more peripheral association with M GmbH in its genesis. The current M550i xDrive, for instance, has both a powerful V-8 engine and all-wheel drive, and can be seen as a sensible halfway house between the standard four- and six-cylinder 5-Series models and the mighty M5, with its 600-plus-horsepower M-fettled engine and chassis. Likewise, the

recent M240i was a version of the compact coupé that fell only slightly short of the barnstorming M2 Competition but still boasted an energetic 335-horsepower straight six and a sports-tuned rear-drive chassis. In earlier years, the M135i designation used to indicate a potent 3-liter straight six and pure rear-wheel drive, but now that the mainstream 1-Series and 2-Series lineups have transitioned to front-wheel-drive platforms, today's M135i packs a 2-liter turbo four, with 306 horsepower and xDrive all-wheel drive. The same basic package propels the larger 2-Series, including the swoopy Gran Coupé.

M Performance is also used for particular accessories and aftermarket components, often to provide sporting upgrades: good examples are add-on spoilers, alternative wheel designs, and high-performance silencer systems.

Diesels Also Welcome Under the M Banner

SUVs and top-end models apply a similar philosophy, and in many cases the M prefix can also allow the presence of diesel-powered models under the M banner. The X5 M50d and X7 M50d were good examples of this: genuinely high-performing diesels that are notable in engineering terms for having featured a power unit with no fewer than four turbochargers. Elsewhere in the lineup, the X3 M40i and X3 M40d, as well as their X4 counterparts, indicate high-line models with gasoline and diesel power, respectively.

Even the limousine 7-Series gained an M tag for a short while. BMW's planners, perhaps controversially, chose the designation M760Li for the very top model in order to signify the presence of a mighty V-12 engine and a skillfully upgraded chassis. But self-evidently, although an impressive performer that handled its near-600 horsepower with great finesse, it was about as far away from a racy M4 as could be imagined.

As the most powerful model in the Z4 range, the Z4 M40i carries M-Performance branding. No full-M version of this Z4 generation (co-developed with Toyota) is offered.

M Division dipped its toe into the luxury segment with the 2017 M760Li xDrive. The turbocharged 609 horsepower V-12 engine was complemented by subtle design tweaks and a chassis carefully calibrated to combine top-level comfort with precise high-speed handling.

Still with today's hierarchy, models with M Sport suffixes have a looser connection with M headquarters in Garching. M Sport is now effectively a series of options or option packs to provide visual enhancements, external and interior, as well as aerodynamic components, firmer suspension, lower ride heights, and wheel, brake, and tire packages. These differ from market to market too.

Confusingly, iPerformance also made an appearance as a BMW sub-brand, serving as the secondary branding for BMW models with hybrid or electrified powertrains. But now that almost every current BMW model has some form of hybridization as standard, the designation has become redundant: regular mild hybrid models go with simple branding like 330i or 530i, while their more expensive, big-batteried plug-in range-mates—in this instance the 330e and 530e—take on a new "e" suffix.

Blasts from the Past: How M Designations Evolved

Historically, it was the very first M535i, dating from 1980, that was responsible for starting the whole roadgoing M-Car bloodline. Despite a designation that would indicate little more than a mildly enhanced standard 5-Series today, the E12-based model was in fact a genuine product of what was then known as BMW Motorsport GmbH. It incorporated far-reaching modifications such as a tuned version of the largest available six-cylinder engine, a close-ratio gearbox, suspension and braking improvements, and an aero bodywork package that looks modest today but was considered extreme in the early 1980s.

That M535i designation carried through into the successor model, the E28. Almost at the same time, the first M5 appeared, complete with its twenty-four-valve M88 engine taken from the race-inspired M1 supercar. In the interim, the big 6-Series coupé had been the first to borrow the M1's engine, becoming the M635i in 1984 and later assuming the M6 nameplate in North America. All these were full-fledged Motorsport engineering programs.

Following the advent of that first M5 in 1985, all core BMW Motorsport GmbH model programs were identified by the letter *M* and a single figure to indicate the model series. But peripheral projects involving motorsport expertise could easily slip in under the radar with an innocently plain-looking designation. The 320iS of the late 1980s was actually a Motorsport-developed version of the legendary E30 M3, but with a special short-stroke engine to shrink the displacement to below 2 liters for tax-break markets like Italy and Portugal. As a testament to the engineers' prowess, the 320iS's power was only marginally down on the equivalent 2.3-liter M3 models. Around the same time, BMW Motorsport GmbH was working on an ultra-high-performance version of the big V-12-powered 850 Ci sports coupé for a planned M8. When that model was canned, many of Motorsport's developments (though not the forty-eight-valve version of the engine) were incorporated without any obvious fuss into the CSi launched in 1992.

The previous-generation M135i is fondly remembered as an enjoyably sporting rear-drive hatchback with a potent straight six engine. Today's equivalent has a turbocharged four-cylinder engine and all-wheel drive.

Though not strictly speaking a product of the M Division, the 2020 128ti revives a classic suffix and shows BMW's expertise in developing a responsive hot hatchback with front-wheel drive.

Inspired by the M Ethos

When it came to driver enjoyment, many other BMW road cars magically hit the spot over the years. Though not direct products of the M Division, they were certainly inspired by the M ethos. Examples include the early 1990s 318iS of the E36 generation, which boasted a delightfully revvy sixteen-valve four-cylinder engine with a then-impressive 140 horsepower. The second generation of the often-derided Compact also included a hidden gem: the 2001 325ti Compact revived the famous ti designation and was the only six-cylinder in that body. With 192 horsepower propelling just 1,400 kilograms, it was an entertaining if short-lived performer.

Much the same spirit was rekindled a generation later with the 2020 128ti. On the face of it, this looked to be an unpromising addition to the front-wheel-drive 1-Series range, and potentially a risky use of the coveted ti label—especially as it was billed as a lower-powered, less lavishly equipped version of the range-topping, all-wheel-drive M135i. But BMW's recipe did the trick: with M-Sport suspension and shorn of the drive to the rear axle, the ti was lighter and more responsive thanks to an expertly tuned chassis and was hailed by commentators as BMW's first hot hatch and a worthy rival to the Golf GTI. It's hard to believe that M-Division experts were not involved on this model somewhere along the line.

Though not officially an M program, it's also hard to believe that M Division did not contribute something to the groundbreaking i8. This supercar-format sports coupé prompted a wholesale rethink of how high-performance vehicles could be powered responsibly into a carbon-conscious future. On its debut in 2013, the flamboyant mid-engined 2+2 seemed to embody all that was exciting about advanced engineering, housing a plug-in hybrid drivetrain within a carbon-fiber chassis and topped by futuristic bodywork with a distinct sci-fi allure. Its headline statistics were impressive for the time, with peak system power of 362 horsepower and 0–100 kilometer-per-hour acceleration in 4.4 seconds. But the most telling figure of all was its CO_2 emissions, some two-thirds lower than that of even a humble family hatchback. Senior BMW managers were all encouraged to run i8s as their personal vehicles, demonstrating that it really was possible to commute to work each day—with considerable glamour and style—on electric power alone, without using a single drop of fuel or emitting a gram of CO_2.

As a vision of the future, it was unquestionably a great success. Throughout its seven-year production lifetime there were persistent rumors of an even faster version, but no M derivative actually materialized. Even so, the i8 remains an eloquent expression of the imagination and the creativity of BMW's future vision, engineering, and design. It assuredly will not be the last.

Inventive minds: by combining a plug-in battery drivetrain with a three-cylinder gasoline engine, the 2013 i8 broke fresh ground as an ecologically responsible supercar.

Landmark designs, from top to bottom: the 1999 Z8 roadster, with engineering elements from the M5; the 1978 M1, which gave the first M Cars their race-bred engines; the 2013 i8, which pioneered plug-in hybrid technology in the supercar segment; and the classic 1955 507 roadster. Only the M1 bears the official stamp of M Division, though all show the imaginative thinking that continues to inspire the M ethos.

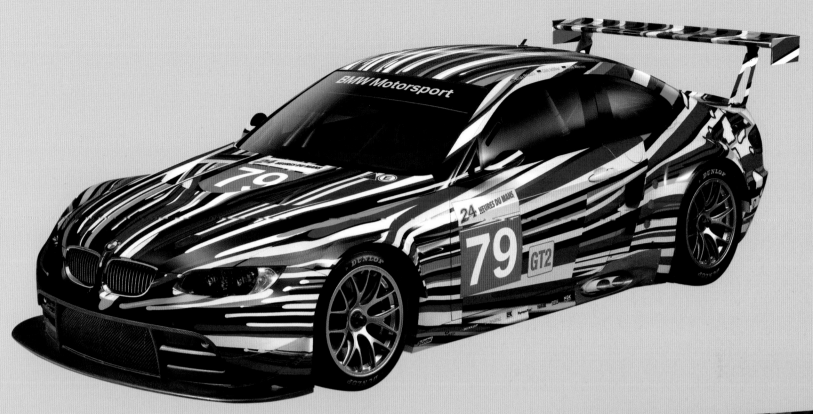

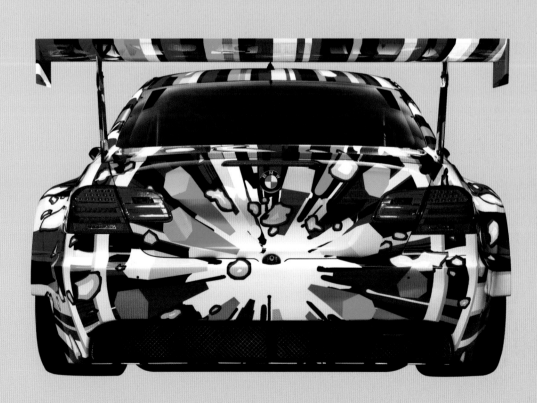

Jeff Koons M3 GT2 Art Car, 24 Hours of Le Mans, 2010

SHAPING THE
M STORY
INSIDE THE DESIGN STUDIO

How does an M Car stand out
from the crowd? Secrets from chief
designer Marcus Syring's studio

14

BMW designers have
risen to the challenge
of finding a fresh form
language to symbolize
the new era of zero-
emission electric
vehicles. This is an
early sketch for the
i4 program.

BMW i Design

BMW i Design

BMW i Design

TO ENTHUSIASTS STEEPED IN sports cars and high-performance car culture it might sound like a strange question, but how *does* an M Car stand out from the crowd? Those aficionados would immediately cite technical parameters such as performance, acceleration, handling, and the like—but what about visual distinctions, the external distinguishing marks that signal the M mechanicals lurking beneath?

The answer, says M-Division chief designer Marcus Syring, is that it depends entirely on the model, and what role it has been assigned in the overall strategy of the division. Every model has a different part to play. For example, as the high-performance business express, the M5 sedan needs to be sleek and discreet. The compact M2 can reflect its more youthful customer base and racing connections with a more extrovert exterior and more dramatic details like spoilers and fancy wheels. The big M-SUVs need to come across as bolder and more aggressive, while a flagship model such as the M8 coupé must convey exclusivity allied with implicit—but not overt—signaling of power and potency.

It wasn't always like that, however, and when BMW Motorsport GmbH first began to gain traction in the 1980s, there was little on the exterior to give the early M Cars away. The first M5, for instance, looked tame in the extreme: only the most knowledgeable car buffs could spot the key details—often just badges—that signified that this was in fact the fastest four-door sedan in the world.

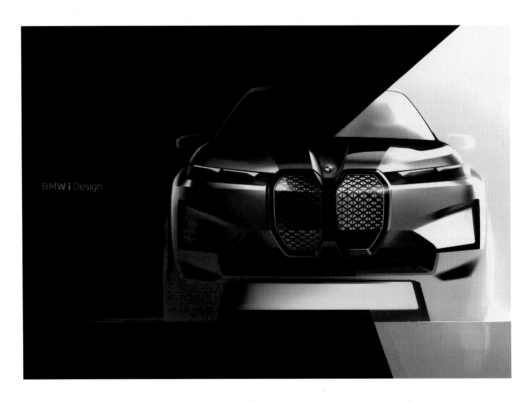

MARCUS SYRING: A man of many designs

Marcus Syring first saw the BMW Z1 sports car as a student, and it was the daring originality of this 1989 two-seater that inspired him to join BMW. As a designer in the Motorsport GmbH offshoot (later BMW M GmbH), he worked on race cars as well as production M Cars such as the E46 M3 and E39 M5. In 1997 he moved to the Technik GmbH advanced design group, and in 2000 he was asked by BMW group design chief Chris Bangle to lead exterior design at Mini.

After three generations of Minis, including the first convertible and the second Clubman, he moved to Rolls-Royce, creating the second-generation Phantom and Ghost, and the new Cullinan. Finally, when BMW reestablished a separate studio for M Cars, Syring was appointed to lead it—even though, by his own admission, he no longer designs cars himself but works with his team of designers to explore ideas and cultivate a climate of creativity.

Syring has worked with Mini and Rolls-Royce as well as BMW.

The BMW Z1 inspired a young Syring to become a car designer.

Syring worked on the legendary E30 M3 race cars early in his twenty-nine-year career at BMW. Even these classics had downplayed their potency, with plain-Jane treatment of body surfaces and detailing to give the impression that aesthetic styling took second place to engineering performance, handling, and efficiency. Recalling how he would have to repair the race cars on Mondays following their competition scrapes the day before, Syring began to capitalize on the already direct link between the roadgoing BMWs and their motorsport counterparts: he went on to design race-influenced details on the successor M3, the E36 model, and later took full responsibility for the Z3 Roadster, the E39 M5, and then one of the most favored M3s of all time, the E46 series that launched in 2000.

Those cars might look tame today, but Syring is quick to point out how the market has changed. "In their day, cars such as the E46 M3 and the E39 M5 did look much sportier [than the regular models]," he says. "But what you see today in the automotive industry is that even small cars with just a few horsepower try to look like race cars, especially at the front: it's constantly ramping up and up, and cars are getting more expressive than they used to be in the past."

Yet, continues the designer, those external trends are not really of such great importance in designing today's M Cars. "We begin by looking at what the car really needs on a technical level. At the front end we look at cooling, and it is cooling requirements that dictate how we design the openings at the front. And, for sure, this will give the car a different graphic—and for an X model it might be bolder and more rugged, while for an M5 it might be sleeker."

While the front-end air intake design is determined by the engine's cooling demand, the designers also have to look at the downforce on the front and rear axles, leading to the placement of flaps and splitters in front of the wheels and a gurney or a spoiler lip on the trunk lid; these also help reduce aerodynamic drag. Next, he says, it is consultations with the engineers on the wheel and track dimensions that are required to achieve the desired lap times around the Nürburgring Nordschleife. These in turn determine the degree of front and rear wheelarch extensions required, while the larger engine may call for a power dome on the hood.

"To start with, the hardpoints are all defined by the physics and technology," he asserts. "By designing it with this emphasis on maximum sporting performance we are also creating a relationship to the race cars. At M we also manage the co-operation with BMW Motorsport in DTM, GTE, and also Formula E cars—and this kind of pure racing design language is something that we can transform into a design language for a production car."

This intimate, almost symbiotic relationship between production cars and race cars is a recurrent theme throughout the activities of M Division. It's one of the key factors that distinguish M Cars from the many imitators that have sprung up hoping to cash in on their acclaim. The ideal for a designer, Syring notes, is when form follows function. "You can see this on the front of an M Car: the technical requirements for cooling and aerodynamics give us a design aesthetic which also signifies that this is a genuinely high-performance car and that it is derived from race cars. This is the best outcome."

▲ BMW M chief designer Marcus Syring: "M-Car styling begins with the model's technical requirements."

▶▶ The production BMW i4, as revealed at the BMW annual general meeting in March 2021. The intensity of the design language is significantly toned down from that of the sketches and the Concept i4 show car.

Controls, displays, and user interfaces will become ever more important as vehicle connectedness increases. BMW's curved display, here seen in the iX, and its latest iDrive system aim to be even more intuitive in readiness for semi and fully autonomous driving in the future.

Asked for a recent example that best illustrates this ethos, Syring without hesitation cites the M2 CS: "The M2 was already a strong design but for the CS we added a front splitter, as well as specific wheels that are lighter and more aerodynamically designed. The M2 CS Racing for customer race series goes even further with a large wing for rear downforce."

The racing car aesthetic can even extend into the world of digitization, electronics, and cockpit displays, as Syring explains: "M GmbH in Garching is always pushing and is never afraid of new technologies—and, for M, digitization is a really fantastic opportunity. Having digital screens allows us to have our own setup, and for the driver this makes it much easier than with the old hardware dials: we can choose the kind of content, the layout, the design, and the color." Among these setups are instrumentation displays that mimic those found in racing cars, appearing when the driver selects the more extreme of the driving modes.

This highly specific M interpretation of the digital world is then combined with analog hardware such as the pedals and the physical mode buttons on the steering wheel for the truly direct touch that is so precious to M customers.

New manufacturing technologies are welcomed by M designers too—and not just the familiar lightweight carbon-fiber composites for roof panels and aerodynamic components. 3D printing is also proving useful for saving weight, and for alloy wheels it unlocks the potential to produce 3D-printed sand-die-cast forms. These, says Syring, allow engineers to design completely different structures that are not just light but also aerodynamic and extremely efficient. Fitted to the M8 GTE, these wheels have hollow spokes, with the hollows only visible from the side. 3D digital milling is another technique with great potential for producing light and highly polished components, he says.

The 2019 Vision iNext show concept (above left) shocked many observers with its aggressive proportions and blocky detailing, but again the production model has been softened to make it more acceptable to the wider audience for all-electric propulsion.

Toward an Electric Future

Looking further ahead, does Syring see electric cars fitting into BMW's M-Car portfolio, and, if so, will such models require a new design language? "I don't see electrification as an obstacle," comes the answer: "I would simply do it. At BMW we have our 'power of choice' strategy offering a range of powertrain types, and we still have combustion engines which will continue for some time. But why not an electrified M Car? After all, we are doing Formula E and we are actually racing electric cars. Also, with BMW SIM racing you can compete with young kids, so we're not afraid of the electrified digital world."

All this, he suggests, could result in an M electrified car that might focus on lateral acceleration—in other words, cornering, yaw response, and maneuverability—and not necessarily aim for peak longitudinal acceleration. "I believe we have great possibilities for the future," he explains. "Yes, we would lose some of our iconic design details, such as the four exhausts—but we'd then be gaining space for a very large diffuser where the muffler and the exhausts used to be: it could be very attractive and expressive. At the front end you will still need a lot of air for cooling the electronics, but maybe in a different position, so it will be up to us to develop our own design language for these new functionally driven details."

In summary, says Syring, the move into electrification is a big opportunity for BMW M and car design in general. It will happen step by step, and two of the designs—the iX and the i4—are already in the public domain.

The 2019 iVision M Next concept gave an early hint of how BMW M design might transition into an electric future. Though showing clear signs of an M1 influence, this model will not be manufactured but its details may influence upcoming e-products.

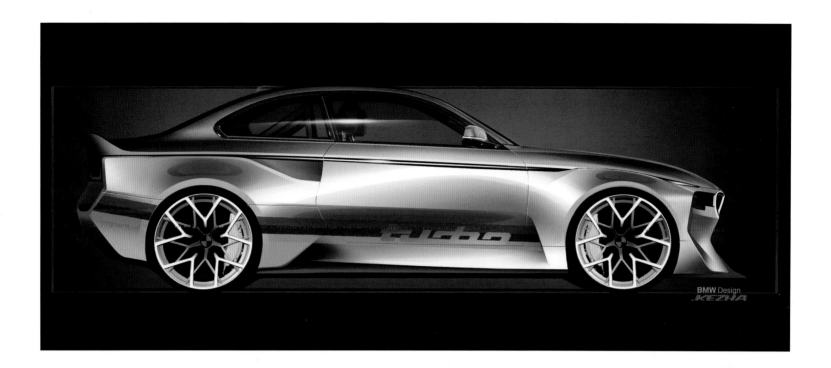

On the perennial question of whether the M Division will develop a car of its own, not based on an existing volume production BMW model, the designer immediately becomes animated. "As a designer, I could imagine something small and light, a bit like the new Alpine or even the Lotus Super Seven; we've already done the M Next showcar, which references our original M1. But what instantly came into my mind was a successor to the 2002 Turbo: a little three-box sedan with lots of power, but electrified in order to transport that idea into the new era of sustainability. Fun without guilt, perhaps."

A show car inspired by the 2002 Turbo has already appeared—Michael Scully's Hommage model from 2016—but Syring stresses that his idea would not be for a retro car but for something done in a modern way and with a strong element of playfulness and desirability. But is there a chance that something like this could pass the cost tests and actually be built? "I'll start tomorrow," he jokes. "If you don't try, you'll never get it."

Within R&D, he reveals, there are "so many ideas" being developed that will never be seen by anyone outside the company. "You have to try and test and think through all these ideas in order to hit upon the right product for the customer. Remember, we are the company that dared to build cars like the Z1, with new materials and ideas like sliding doors. We built the i8, too. So maybe there *is* a small chance—and perhaps this could be the starting point."

An early sketch for Michael Scully's 2016 Hommage concept celebrating the 2002 Turbo of the 1970s. Something "small and light" like this is what current design chief Syring believes could be an exciting project for the new era of fun without guilt.

INSIDE M-DIVISION'S DESIGN STUDIO

Hive of activity: BMW's design studios undertake everything from the initial inspiration sketches to full-scale clay models, ergonomic and interface innovation and color, material, and trim selection for concept cars and production models.

TODAY, TOMORROW
AND INTO AN ELECTRIC FUTURE

CEO Markus Flasch on why zero-emission M Cars will deliver even more thrills

15

The iVision Dynamics showcar concept from 2017 was instrumental in exploring a new design language for next-generation battery-powered BMW models.

Markus Flasch, head of BMW M Division: "At M, we see electrification as an opportunity with huge potential benefits."

BY ANY MEASURE—be it commercial, technical, or in terms of innovation and influence—the advance of BMW's M Division over the last half-century has been spectacular. The founding fathers in the 1960s—a small group of highly talented engineers—soon morphed into the nucleus of a racing team that came to dominate European Touring Car racing, channeling vital racetrack experience back into BMW road cars to push them further ahead of the competition year after year. As we have seen, that productive feedback loop would lead to some fabulous road cars such as the 3.0 CSi, as well as the exotic M1 supercar and, of course, the first directly Motorsport-influenced series production car, the M635 CSi.

With many other automakers, a moment's success in competition can produce a brief flurry of reflected glory in the sales charts, only for the energy from that racetrack flirtation to evaporate without a trace. By contrast, BMW engineers have pushed this race-road symbiosis hard and without pause throughout those fifty years. That core ethos, providing a tangible, hardwired link between race car and road car, is what has helped BMW's M operation to connect so directly—and so profitably—to its growing legions of loyal customers and hard-core fans.

Taking that seminal M635 CSi's 1984 debut year and its roughly fourteen hundred early-adopter buyers as our baseline, M Division's figures have expanded more than thirty-fold to today's consistent annual sales of forty- or forty-five thousand units. That figure rises to over one-hundred-and-forty thousand if we widen the net to include noncore M-Performance models like the M135i and M535i xDrive. The M Division's right foot has almost never come off the gas, the only dips in the relentlessly rising sales graph being due to external factors such as two global economic crises and the timing of certain key model replacement cycles.

The key drivers throughout have been the most highly focused models of all, those that have done the most to define the M brand: the M3 and, since 2014, the M4 coupé into which the M3's boundary-pushing DNA was transfused. Each new generation of the M3/M4 has prompted an uptick in production as eager buyers place their orders, most notably in the early 2000s, when the excitement around the E46 generation was at its peak and annual output surged past twenty-five thousand for the first time. This was also the time when M GmbH was in the throes of reshaping itself into a genuine multimodel operation, adding significant numbers of Z3 M Roadsters and Coupés as well as the pricey M6 Grand Tourers. Prior to the millennium, the range had been that of the original M3 plus M5 pairing, and thus strongly geared around the development and replacement cycles for these two models.

The near doubling of production numbers that occurred between 2014 and 2019 is often attributed to the spiraling success of the still-contentious SUVs and their M versions. That is perhaps true, but it must also be remembered that the overall sales of regular BMW-brand models were climbing steeply at the same time, and that the heroic compact M2 was beginning to make a strong impression, too—at times it equated to almost one in eight 2-Series models built. While the launch of the X5M and X6M in 2009 did reveal significant demand for high-powered 4x4s (and indeed contrived to open up a whole new market subsector), the percentage of X-segment buyers choosing M models is significantly less. For the X5M, demand typically maxes out at below 3 percent, while for the more rakish coupé-style X6M the figure is understandably higher. The more recent X3M and X4M show a similar disparity, at around 2 and 6 percent, respectively.

All in all, the SUVs together typically contribute around a quarter of aggregate core M-Model sales, with the M3 and M5 each at about one-eighth: the top performers are the M4 and M2, each at around the one-fifth mark. In combination, these represent a powerful and assuredly profitable portfolio, but also a somewhat unbalanced one. By relentlessly chasing power and performance, the company has fielded vehicles whose power and cost have grown together exponentially; even the M2, brought in expressly to attract younger and less-moneyed buyers, now costs between twice and three times as much as that other popular performance icon, the VW Golf GTI. Would the launch of lower-cost M Cars, perhaps based on the front-wheel-drive architecture of the modern 1- and 2-Series, risk diluting the M brand? M GmbH CEO Markus Flasch, in an interview for this book, was quick to rule out such a venture—but not on the grounds of brand dilution. With only around 1 percent of all BMWs being pure M models, he doesn't see that as a risk. "We don't see this happening," he commented firmly. "Front-wheel drive is not in the character of M, and for us the minimum would be all-wheel drive." Those fond of reading between the lines will note that this does not exclude an all-wheel-drive setup along the lines of that used by the M135i xDrive, but with its bias directed more toward the rear wheels, as in larger models like the M4. It is possible, too, that the current M2 may get a replacement that retains the rear-wheel drive that its fans so covet, so there's certainly an opportunity for a compact but perhaps less extreme and better-priced entrypoint to the M range.

(CONTINUES ON PAGE 212)

M-Division 50th birthday snapshot, spring 2021: the first M-branded supersports bike, the M 1000 RR, takes pride of place between the sixth-generation M3 sedan and the latest edition of the M4 Coupé.

M TAKES TO TWO WHEELS

The first M-branded BMW supersports bike is released: welcome the 212-horsepower, 15,100 rpm M 1000 RR

Envious of M-Car drivers and their enjoyment of high-performance road cars directly influenced by the racetrack experience, motorcycle enthusiasts have long pressed for the two-wheeled equivalent of an M2 or M4. With BMW having fielded a frontline works team in the World Superbike Championships since 2009, the company's top motorcycle engineers possess the perfect mechanism for technology transfer from track to street.

Top-line supersports road bikes are far closer to racing machinery than are their four-wheeled counterparts, so it made sense for the M 1000 RR to be based on the highly regarded S 1000 RR, BMW's top performance road bike—and the model ridden by Tom Sykes and his teammates in the World Superbike Championship. Just as with M Division's cars, the M 1000 RR is aimed at customers "with particularly high demands relating to performance, exclusiveness, and individuality"—so a suite of upgrades to the engine, chassis, suspension, and braking raises the machine's game significantly.

The four-cylinder RR-based engine shifts strongly toward racing practice with new forged two-ring pistons, titanium conrods, polished inlet ports, and a 13.5:1 compression ratio. With the safe rev range extended to 15,100 rpm, the 1-liter unit produces no less than 212 horsepower at 14,500 rpm, exceeding the RR's figures from 6,000 rpm upward. The chassis still uses conventional aluminum (even though BMW had earlier developed a carbon frame for the HP4 Race), but the geometry is uncompromisingly that of a race bike, with braking and anti-squat control to maximize the feedback loop between rider and wheels. The wheels themselves are carbon and the powerful brakes carry M branding.

A particularly impressive aspect is the clear interplay between advanced aerodynamics and aesthetic design to produce a machine that is stylish and eye-catching as well as efficient on the racetrack. Double winglets on each side of the fairing serve to generate downforce as speeds rise: this helps in both the braking and

The M 1000 RR uses racetrack expertise to push the performance envelope still further. The production-based engine uses exotic materials to extract 212 horsepower at 14,500 rpm from just 1,000cc, while the competition-inspired chassis, brakes, and streamlining help optimize downforce and grip for rapid circuit lap times.

the acceleration phases to generate quicker lap times. Under braking, more load is applied to the front wheel for improved retardation, while acceleration performance is boosted as the downforce helps keep the front wheel on the ground and also adds load to the rear tire. This in turn improves traction and, as a result, minimizes traction-control interventions to enable the transfer of maximum power to the road for more of the time.

Indeed, even on the street version, the M's statistics mark it out as a bike for very serious enthusiasts: ready to ride, it weighs just 192 kilograms, hits 100 kilometers per hour in fractionally over 3 seconds, and goes on to top the 300 kilometer-per-hour mark.

Just as in the four-wheeled M models, electronics play a major part in enhancing the performance of the M 1000 RR and adapting its characteristics to suit the rider's preferences, whether on the racetrack or the public road. No fewer than seven riding modes—Rain, Road, Dynamic, Race, and Race Pro 1 through 3—work in conjunction with the latest traction and wheelie control functions and a six-axis sensor. There are even a pit-lane speed limiter and a large 6.5-inch TFT instrument cluster, which is capable of displaying lap times and sector times.

Again in parallel with the M Cars, an M Competition Package is available for the new model, adding further carbon and milled aluminum elements, a lighter swingarm, and the maintenance-free M-Endurance final drive chain. Given a totally free hand, BMW M engineers would certainly have added a still higher level of sophistication to the M 1000 RR's specifications, but World Superbike regulations stipulate a maximum showroom price of €40,000 for the street model—a figure the new BMW bike is expected to comfortably undercut.

M Division is extending its thinking into the supersports motorcycle sector with the M 1000 RR, revealed in 2020.

BMW chief executive Oliver Zipse introduces the Concept i4 prototype in an online presentation in 2020. The following year he revealed to shareholders that the company would also be complementing the production battery-powered crossover with an M-Performance edition, making it the first electric model to receive the attention of BMW's M Division.

(CONTINUED FROM PAGE 209)

Looking Ahead

It has not gone unnoticed at BMW's M Division that the international establishment, along with a growing slice of the world's car buyers, has fallen out of love with the internal combustion engine—the device that is at the very heart of M's business model and key to the appeal of every one of its models. The Paris Agreement on climate change has now been ratified by almost every nation on earth, more than a hundred countries have committed to net-zero carbon targets by 2050, and scores of markets have announced the outlawing of gasoline- and diesel-engined cars during—or even in advance of—the 2030s. Does that not pose an existential threat to everything that M produces?

A greeting card popular around the turn of the millennium showed a tortuous mountain road snaking across a lofty pass from one treacherous hairpin bend to the next; the message inside carried wording to the effect that "a bend in the road is only the end of the road if you fail to take the turn." On the evidence of the past half-century, BMW's M engineers have proved themselves supremely adept at negotiating the many seemingly scary turns that have cropped up in the course of their itinerary: migrating to turbocharged engines in the face of protests from the M fan base; convincing enthusiasts that automatic transmissions can deliver greater driver satisfaction than manuals, and proving that four-wheel drive can be entertaining as well as enhancing safety.

Clearly, M-Division CEO Markus Flasch is under no illusions; the challenge of weaning avowed car fanatics off their gasoline diet is several orders of magnitude greater than that of persuading loyal customers that one type of transmission is better than another. But he remains undaunted, approaching this looming threat with a confidence bordering on equanimity, emboldened by the singular advantage that the BMW parent company is already a front-runner in electrification, battery technology, and the development of all the associated electronic control systems. After all, BMW was the first automaker to launch a dedicated electric car, the i3, and the first into the supercar segment with a plug-in hybrid, the i8—a genuine groundbreaker, though not developed directly by M GmbH.

Despite this corporate groundswell of electrical expertise, at the time of writing no production M Car has yet seen fit to incorporate any element of hybridization or electrification; the purity of the driving experience is the overriding priority, and hybrids do not yet appear to cut it. Yet, says Flasch, M engineers are already on the case: "At M, we see electrification as an opportunity, and we are exploring plug-in as well as battery electric, and we see this mostly in an all-wheel-drive configuration. But we're not looking at [simpler] technologies like add-on electric rear axles."

Instead, clarifies Flasch, there are already electrified models in development. He is quick to call out the huge potential benefits that will ensure that future electrified M models stay faithful to the M Division's golden rule, that the successor model must always outperform its predecessor. But underlying his affirmation is a clear message: M will not necessarily tread the same path as several other manufacturers, whose early 2020s electric models have packed huge amounts of horsepower for headline-grabbing straightline acceleration at the expense of weight and handling agility.

"Yes, of course there is acceleration, and that's easy," says Flasch, "but that's not the only attribute that M Cars need. Power boosting is interesting, for sure, but I see electrification giving M the potential for differentiation more in the area of transversal dynamics, driving dynamics, recuperation, braking, chassis control. This is where we will make the difference."

For M, he stresses, outperforming has never been merely a matter of longitudinal performance. The overall character, the overall dynamics must be superior—that is what counts. Here, the transition to electric power can definitely help: technologies such as torque vectoring can add a whole new dimension to chassis control, and on Flasch's own admission there is "so much still unexplored" when it comes to the dynamic possibilities opened up by braking and recuperation strategies.

Does that mean an all-electric M model is likely to emerge? "Absolutely," responds Flasch with no hesitation whatsoever. "We're already working on it, and it's a question of when, rather than if. At the moment we've got a fantastic model lineup: our cars perform very well, they are popular and they sell, so there is no need for us to rush into one technology or the other just for the sake of fashion. But we are keeping our eyes open and pushing ahead with development and just waiting for the right time. So, yes, I do see a fully electric M Car: the question is simply when."

When it comes to specifics, however, the M GmbH CEO is understandably less forthcoming. Looking uncannily like an amalgam of the original M1 and the 2013 i8, the 2019 Vision M Next supercar concept has been held up by many as a possibility for production as the first standalone M Car since the iconic M1. Yet, counters Flasch, it is just that: a concept car that gives some ideas of what the design of future M Cars might look like, including some details. "But overall, it remains a concept car and there is no close connection to any derivatives that we are planning," he states firmly.

(CONTINUES ON PAGE 216)

Welcome to the new electric age: M Division's signature technology has always been ultrasophisticated internal combustion engines, but it has high-performance ideas at the ready for the super sporting electric cars of the future.

BMW INDIVIDUAL

Where performance and limited-edition works of art meet personalization and bespoke craftsmanship

Sharing facilities with BMW's M operation is BMW Individual, which specializes in creating bespoke hand-crafted interiors and special exterior treatments for discerning customers.

To understand the full importance of this activity within BMW M's Garching operations, just refer to its title in German—*BMW Individual Manufaktur*—where the last word conveys the notion of handcrafting or personalized design, equipment, and finishes. When the division was formed in 1992, global demand for bespoke enhancements on regular production cars was minimal and the range of choices within each nameplate was so narrow as to be meaningless. But that has all changed in the intervening three decades; today there are so many factory-fit options on every manufacturer's price list that within each model range scarcely any two cars leaving the factory are identical in every respect.

BMW helped kick off this trend and popularized it in a big way from 2001 on when the Mini became the first small car that could be personalized by every buyer.

Yet for some customers even this vastly expanded spectrum of options for paint, upholstery, wheel designs, graphics, and decor themes was still not enough to provide the required level of personalization and exclusivity. For them, the BMW Individual service can develop a truly tailor-made vehicle, by definition a one-off. Nothing is off-limits, save changes that might affect the car's structure or safety.

The main areas where customers like to show their individuality are in bespoke fabrics and trim materials, wood and carbon interior panels, and special paint finishes—including innovative matte, semi-matte, and sinister "stealth" Vantablack coatings that absorb light to make the car nearly invisible under certain conditions. The "Frozen" paint finishes have been particularly popular with customers for the X5M and X6M ranges.

"BMW Individual is like an add-on business to our traditional performance-oriented work," says M CEO Markus Flasch. "It is growing, and we expect it to grow even faster in future. It will come to play a bigger role: we have done some interesting things in the past, and now we have done a cooperation with an artist in New York. There will be more of those, too."

These artistic collaborations represent an important step forward for BMW Individual: first, they mark a symbolic connection with the famous BMW Art Cars of the past, and, second, they are not one-offs destined for museums or private collections—instead, they're manufactured in much larger (though still limited) series and can be bought by any customer. The first of these, appearing in early 2020, was the all-black M2 Competition Edition, developed in conjunction with the New York artist Futura 2000 and

featuring specific components such as the bumpers, side skirts, and interior carbon inset panels individually hand-painted by the artist, thus ensuring that no two examples are exactly alike.

As a follow-up later that year, the all-new 2021 M4 received the Individual art treatment too: again drawing on American street culture, the M4 Competition x Kith emerged out of a close collaboration between the automaker and the New York designer Ronnie Fieg and his Kith label. Finished in a choice of three different matte "Frozen" shades, the hundred-and-fifty-unit limited edition includes carbon-fiber trims for exterior features such as the air intakes and spoilers, a revised co-branded Kith-BMW roundel on the hood, and a carbon roof with gray Kith lettering woven into the carbon fabric of the roof surface.

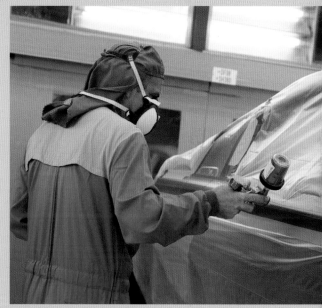

"The collaboration with fashion designer Ronnie Fieg and Kith is a great opportunity for BMW M to bridge the gap between the original BMW M3 and our new BMW M4 Competition Coupé from the sixth generation of this iconic model series," says Markus Flasch. "The contemporary fashion scene is changing from a cultural phenomenon to a global lifestyle attitude, bringing a new and very distinctive brand of exclusivity to many different areas."

◤ The artist Futura 2000, who previously went under the name Leonard Hilton McGurr, at work on his limited-edition series of M2 CS coupés.

▶ The artist and BMW M CEO Markus Flasch at the launch of the limited-edition M2 CS by Futura 2000 at Paramount Pictures Studios in Hollywood in February 2020.

iVision M Next: the plug-in hybrid supercar concept from 2019 was inspired by the production M1 from the 1970s. But M CEO Flasch says that it will not form the basis of a new standalone M model.

(CONTINUED FROM PAGE 213)

Flexible Architectures Give BMW Buyers the Power of Choice

On the other hand, there's a good deal more clarity in relation to BMW's principal model ranges and how they might yield additional M models. Many, if not most, of the main volume model lines already include plug-in hybrid versions, and before long these will be complemented by fully electrified editions with the same architecture: the battery-powered 2020 iX3 SUV is a good example, and the 3-Series, 5-Series, and big 7-Series are expected to follow suit before long. The secret is the flexible CLAR platform, which allows BMW its much-touted "power of choice" philosophy of providing either gasoline, diesel, plug-in hybrid, or pure electric powertrains across its key nameplates.

It is still open to speculation whether future incarnations of the staple M Cars—the M3, M4, and M5—may be offered with the choice of either Power PHEV plug-in hybrid or pure battery drivetrains. But M Division's immediate focus is likely to be on the all-new shapes that herald the BMW parent marque's broadside entry into the electric-car market and its battle against a strongly advancing Tesla. High-profile, high-performance versions of these new EV ambassadors will be essential if electric power is to be established as a credible option in the M universe.

For the 2022 model year, BMW will launch its i4, a mainstream electric crossover aimed at competing with the Tesla Model 3. The "standard" i4 already packs some 500-plus horsepower, according to BMW, and Flasch confirms that an M-Performance version is in the pipeline—though he declines to say whether it will carry a full M designation or be labeled i4M. Slightly ahead of the i4 on the launch list is the larger and more futuristic iX, which will be packed with advanced technologies, including autonomous driving when required. With twin e-motors and ample space for large batteries, it promises considerable scope for the M treatment, not least as a more eco-friendly replacement for the prodigiously powerful, but also unfashionably thirsty, X5M and X6M.

For many M fans, the most burning issue of all remains the long-running, on-off saga of whether there will be an all-new tailor-made M Car, a standalone halo model exclusive to M Division and not based on any series-production BMW. The M1 looms large in every M fan's mind; the model kicked off the whole fantastic M adventure in 1978. It was just such a one-off design, and there hasn't been anything like it since. However, the economics and logistics of such small-run projects are notoriously tricky, and the idea of an elitist extreme performance machine goes against the M-Division ethos of offering a much broader clientele high-performance versions of existing models at more accessible prices.

Even so, Flasch does reveal that BMW is indeed "pursuing development" of a new car that will be M only. "We're working on something that is not based on a standard BMW model," he confirms, "but I can't say anything about the size or the segment. It will be a surprise!"

With M GmbH set to mark its half-century of operation in May 2022, who would bet against the M engineers celebrating those fifty fabulous years with a dramatic new model, one unique to the brand and that, true to the M vision, points the way to an exciting high-tech future rather than harking back to the glories of the past, however great those glories may have been?

Electric Cars: How Can They Satisfy the Famously Demanding M Driver?

On a more technical level, any future hybrid or battery-electric M Car will have quite a mountain to climb if it is to stand tall in the pantheon of M's greats and, perhaps an even bigger challenge, if it is to be accepted with open arms by M GmbH's famously demanding driving enthusiasts.

▼ Full-range electrification: from production hatchbacks and supercars to premium scooters and plug-in hybrid executive sedans, BMW is keen to highlight its big push into battery power.

Facing the future: the production-specification i4 (right) and the SUV-format iX (opposite) will be the ambassadors for the next generation of battery-powered BMW models. High-performance M versions will be essential if BMW is to maintain its market position as a provider of cars that are fast and fun to drive.

To satisfy an M driver, an engine has to feel sharp and incisive and make just the right sounds. The transmission—whether automatic or manual—must shift quickly and positively and with a pleasingly mechanical feel, and the brake pedal must deliver both powerful stopping for fast-driving confidence and progressive retardation for smoothness in everyday traffic. Then there are the many additional parameters close to M drivers' hearts, such as steering weight, feel and gearing, yaw response, suspension and damper tuning, oversteer and understeer balance, throttle sensitivity, and much more.

Anyone who has driven an early-generation electric or hybrid car will know that all these areas are notoriously tricky for the e-engineer to negotiate successfully. Hybrids need careful calibration to blend the power flows of the gasoline engine and electric motor smoothly at all speeds and at all points on the load map; crisp throttle response characteristics are key to the enjoyment of any performance car, most especially an M Car.

Still more critical, perhaps, is brake pedal feel and response. Electric cars rely on a blend of electric retardation—to recuperate energy—and friction braking through conventional discs. Some of today's electric cars have brake pedals that respond sharply if the battery needs top-up energy or more sluggishly if the battery is full and no recuperation is needed at that moment. For M drivers, who demand absolute precision and predictability in the car's responses to their control inputs, such inconsistent braking reactions are simply unacceptable—and the same applies to inconsistencies in all the other aspects of a vehicle's dynamic behavior.

In the high-performance culture that is BMW M GmbH, every designer and engineer lives and breathes these dynamic values and is acutely conscious of the challenge represented by this far-reaching reshaping of the automobile. It is a reset of fundamental values that demands no less than the complete reinvention of the car's most vital (and for M, its most character-defining) core elements—but without diluting the driver experience the vehicle is able to provide.

The task is a daunting one, and one that's critical to the survival of performance-car culture into the zero-carbon era that will soon be upon us. But if there is anyone capable of succeeding in this enterprise of safeguarding the thrill of driving for future generations, it will be BMW M GmbH—as its fifty-year track record of crafting fabulous driving machines so eloquently demonstrates.

ACKNOWLEDGMENTS

ALTHOUGH THIS BOOK WAS COMMISSIONED and planned well before the fateful first case of COVID-19 in Asia in December 2019, everything else involved in the book's production took place under the conditions of a global pandemic and the various periods of total lockdown that affected everyone's lives over the next eighteen months.

For my purposes as the author, this called for a near-total change of plans. Trips to Germany to interview key figures in the BMW M GmbH business were canceled, replaced by Zoom-style meetings. Visits to BMW Welt and the company's extensive classic car collection were put on indefinite hold, and the BMW Archive's numerous treasures had to be examined online rather than in person. Closer to home, another of my ambitious plans also came to nothing: I had thought to visit several of the UK's growing network of brilliantly professional M-Car specialists for some hands-on time—and miles—in the company of many of the older M models, just to refresh my impressions of their dynamics and their special feel on the road. COVID-19 put paid to that idea, too, but I would still like to salute super-knowledgeable outfits like Munich Legends and Classic Heroes for their openness to cooperation—and for their endlessly fascinating blogs, videos, and postings.

With my travel restricted, I thought it wise to supplement my own often still-vivid driving impressions of pivotal BMW M models from bygone decades with counterpoint opinions from my journalist colleagues at leading automotive publications. So here is my roll call of appreciation for the online resources and writerly integrity of *Car*, *Top Gear*, *Autocar*, *Evo*, *Motor Sport*, and other magazines. The website www.bmw.registry.com has been a particularly fastidious and useful resource.

But my most heartfelt thanks must go to two individuals and one big organization for their key contributions to the development of this book.

Motorsport legend and inspirer-in-chief of the whole M-Car adventure, Jochen Neerpasch, kindly agreed to write the foreword—albeit in German, so any faults in translation are mine.

I am also grateful to my colleague Jesse Crosse, who did not take much persuasion to submit his vivid driving impressions from behind the wheel of his treasured M3 CSL. I was as excited to read his words as he was to write them, so thank you again, Jesse.

As for the big organization, that is clearly BMW itself, and in particular hardworking PR-fixers like Martin Harrison in the UK—especially for his sterling work collating official M-Car production figures since the 1970s. I should also mention BMW Group Classic Motorsport, and BMW Group Innovations & Design Communications. Thanks, too, to the senior BMW executives who spared me the time for Zoom interviews, and to the tirelessly patient Ruth Standfuss of BMW Group Archive, who helped source many of the earlier images in the book, some of which I had never seen before.

To the other clients and organizations I write for, I should apologize for the many "I'm sorry—too busy finishing a book" email responses I must have sent.

And finally, I must acknowledge the patience and tolerance of my family, not just with the whole lockdown situation but also with my many lengthy writing sessions locked away in my own private world of M Cars, however engrossing that may have been for me.

—Tony Lewin, March 2021

BIBLIOGRAPHY

Sources

Arron, Simon and Mark Hughes.
  The Complete Book of Formula 1.
  St. Paul, MN: Motorbooks, 2003.

Katalog der Automobil-Revue,
  1989–2013. FMM Fachmedien
  Mobil AG, Bern.

Tony Lewin. *The BMW Century: The
  Ultimate Performance Machines*.
  Minneapolis, MN: Motorbooks,
  2016.

———. *The Complete Book of BMW:
  Every Model since 1950*.
  St. Paul, MN: Motorbooks, 2004.

Mönnich, Horst. *The BMW Story:
  A Company in Its Time*. Translated
  by Anthony Bastow and William
  Henson. London: Sidgwick &
  Jackson, 1991.

Taylor, James. *BMW M3: The Complete
  Story*. Ramsbury, Marlborough:
  The Crowood Press, 2014.

Reference Materials

Auto, motor und sport
www.auto-motor-und-sport.de

Autocar magazine
www.autocar.co.uk

Automobil Revue
www.automobilrevue.ch

BMW M1 club
www.bmw-m1-club.de

Car magazine
www.carmagazine.co.uk

Evo magazine
www.evo.co.uk

Motor Sport magazine
www.motorsportmagazine.com

Race Engine Technology magazine
www.highpowermedia.com

Racecar Engineering magazine
www.racecar-engineering.com

Top Gear magazine
www.topgear.com

www.bmwblog.com

www.bmw.registry.com

www.ultimatespecs.com

www.automobile-catalog.com

www.bmwgroup.com

www.bmwgroup-classic.com

www.historischesarchiv.bmw.de

Specifications Table Notes:

Model code, engine code:
Designations used by BMW internally.

Years in production:
These figures were provided by BMW directly, so they would include early production units built before the model's official launch date.

Number built:
Official figures provided by BMW in Germany.

Launch price:
Approximate tax-paid price, in Germany or the UK, of model when first launched, converted into euros for pre-1999 models. Standard conversion rates of 1 euro = DM 1.9558 and £0.83 have been employed throughout. For current models the German price is given.

Peak power, torque:
Official figures given by BMW.

Performance figures:
Official BMW factory figures or, where not available, figures from reputable independent magazine road tests.

Curb weight:
Official figures given by BMW or best estimates where these are not available. Note: conventions for measuring vehicle weights have changed over the years, so earlier figures may not be comparable with more recent ones.

Maximum speeds:
Some BMW M models from about 2010 onward could be specified with M Driver's Pack allowing the 250-kilometer-per-hour speed limiter to be disabled. This is the second figure quoted.

INDEX